ORIANA AND AURORA
Taking UK cruising into a new millennium

Sharon Poole & Andrew Sassoli-Walker

AMBERLEY PUBLISHING

First published 2012

Amberley Publishing Plc
The Hill, Stroud
Gloucestershire, GL5 4EP

www.amberley-books.com

Copyright © Sharon Poole & Andrew Sassoli-Walker, 2012

The right of Sharon Poole & Andrew Sassoli-Walker to be identified as the Authors
of this work has been asserted in accordance with the Copyrights, Designs and
Patents Act 1988.

ISBN 978 1 4456 0442 8

British Library Cataloguing in Publication Data.
A catalogue record for this book is available from the British Library.

Typeset in 10pt on 13pt Celeste.
Typesetting by Amberley Publishing.
Printed in the UK.

CONTENTS

PREFACE

Oriana (1995) and *Aurora* (2000) were the first new ships commissioned for a British cruise line in over thirty years and the last two cruise liners built for the Peninsular & Oriental Steam Navigation Company before it was demerged and the cruise division purchased by the multi-national Carnival Corporation. There was of course the contemporary, almost futuristic *Royal Princess* built in 1984, but she was designed for P&O's Princess brand and the rapidly expanding North American market and was based on the West Coast of the USA during the summer operating cruises to Alaska, and in the Caribbean during the winter.

For the British there is a degree of romance attached to a sea voyage, even nowadays when cruising has become so much more accessible to many people. While enjoying the relaxation and exploration that go with a cruise, one can become attached to the ambience and style of a particular ship. This was the situation for hundreds of passengers on P&O's venerable liner *Canberra*. It was not therefore an easy task to design not one, but two new vessels, which would, in time, directly replace this much-loved ship. In the event the teams of designers, naval architects, engineers and many other unsung workers succeeded spectacularly and *Oriana* and *Aurora* have both become as popular with UK cruisers as their illustrious predecessor, *Canberra*.

Oriana is the longest serving ship in the current P&O Cruises fleet and, at the time of her building, was the largest and fastest liner built for a quarter of a century. She was also the first cruise ship designed and built specifically for the needs and preferences of P&O Cruises' overwhelmingly British passenger base. *Aurora* followed five years later, her design reflecting lessons learnt from *Oriana*, as well as changes in passengers' expectations

Opposite: Aurora passes *Oriana* in Southampton, their distinctive bow profiles making them easily recognisable. (*Andrew Sassoli-Walker*)

and wishes over the intervening years. In respect of their individual, one-off designs, *Oriana* and *Aurora* are the last of their kind. Nowadays, given the economies of scale in a global market and the consequent growth in demand, P&O Cruises has utilised the Vista and Grand Class hull designs of the shipyard Fincantieri. These have been used over many Carnival brands, most notably Princess Cruises for the Grand Class and Holland America and Cunard Lines for the Vista Class. Although similar in design, each brand adapts varying layouts and décor to suit them and their passengers.

Oriana and *Aurora* both feature traditional wrap-around promenade decks with attractive tiered sterns offering plenty of the open deck space so appreciated by the sun-starved British. Once among the largest cruise ships of their day, they are now classed as mid-size ships at 69,000 and 76,000 tons respectively, each carrying just under 2,000 passengers. Their white hulls, buff funnels and distinctive silhouettes are instantly recognisable all over the world. This is their story ... so far.

On 3 July 2012, P&O Cruises held a Grand Event to celebrate 175 years of their heritage. For the first time, all seven ships of the fleet were in Southampton together. A day of festivities included the Princess Royal and other dignitaries lunching on board *Oriana*. At 17.30 hrs, the ships began to leave port and process down Southampton Water to Spithead for a Review of the Fleet. The vessels broke into two lines, and as each passed THV *Patricia*, the Princess Royal, on board in her capacity as Master of The Corporation of Trinity House, took the salute. The photograph shows *Aurora* and *Oriana* with THV *Patricia*. (*Sharon Poole*)

FOREWORD

ORIANA

It was a great privilege to be selected by the then Chairman of P&O, Lord Sterling of Plaistow GCVO, CBE, to assist in the building of, and to take subsequent command of, the new superliner *Oriana*.

This vessel was the first of a fleet of passenger liners that would change the shape of British-based cruising for the next generation. It was a daunting responsibility for all of us who were involved in the Gemini Project, for such was its codename before the final name was selected. A team of senior personnel, both ship and shore staff, was assembled in Lower Saxony in the small village of Papenburg to supervise the construction. Working together with the family shipbuilding firm of Meyer Werft, headed up by Bernard Meyer, the 69,000 ton liner took shape daily, and metamorphosed into an object of great beauty.

I had been made Commodore of the fleet some months before, and the proudest moment of my seagoing career was at the handover by the yard on completion, when the German flag was lowered and I could raise the P&O Cruises Commodore's standard at the masthead. This was joined by the personal flag of the Chairman, and they both proudly fluttered in the stiff breeze as we left German waters – a significant moment in P&O's long history – a brand new purpose-built cruise liner which would enter the fleet in fine style after the naming ceremony by HM the Queen in April 1995.

Oriana's iconic predecessor *Canberra* had been under my command on and off for many years, and it was with pleasure that I was able to ensure that a number of features of this 1961 British-built ship could be incorporated into *Oriana*'s design. Such was the loyalty of the *Canberra* passengers that they needed something with which to associate their previous cruising experiences, as they were fiercely of the belief that nothing could quite replace their favourite ship. I can truthfully record that she measured up to our and their expectations, and with a team of highly professional and personable officers and crew members, she fully assumed the mantle of Flagship of the Line within months of coming into service.

Anderson's Bar – an intimate area of relaxation, the show lounges, a large and comfortable theatre and two splendid restaurants, the Peninsular and the Oriental, which impressed on all the value of P&O's historical significance.

Coupled with what the passengers saw was the cutting-edge navigational and high-tech engineering heart of the ship, which, although not visible to them, ensured their comfort and safety. Computers which linked satellite navigation to the required engine revolutions to ensure on-time arrivals at ports, joystick control of the main engines, bow and stern thrusters, variable pitch propellers and twin rudders all required technical expertise of the highest calibre, and I was indeed fortunate that the Chief Engineering Officer Marcus James, and the Chief Officer Hamish Reid, were on hand to supply me with incomparable support. That went also for the hand-selected hotel staff who were as welcoming as one could wish, and able to produce vast quantities of nourishment at all times of the day and night.

It goes without saying that had *Oriana* not been an instant and unqualified success, there wouldn't have been an *Aurora* or a subsequent fleet of fine new liners.

The P&O sword with which I was presented by the Chairman before Her Majesty on Naming Day is splendidly and proudly mounted on a bulkhead close to the Pursers Bureau, and one day I will surely be able to reclaim it – but not, I hope, before many more years of excellent service.

It was particularly gratifying that there was almost exclusive use of British products in the décor, installed by British craftsman who took German residence for months. The quality of the carpentry, carpeting and the ambience created by these high standards was immediately obvious on boarding the vessel, and has stood the test of time.

The elegance of the public rooms, particularly the Curzon Room, was highly impressive, and endeared itself to the clientele. There was

Commodore Ian Gibb (Rtd), March 2012

Opposite: Oriana is greeted by fireboats and small craft as she arrives at Sydney for the first time as part of her maiden world cruise, 1996. (P&O Cruises)

Above: Oriana's name stands proud at the base of her funnel. (*David Raymonde*)

Opposite: Aurora, approaching the Upper Swinging Ground as she arrives home at Southampton on a still summer morning. (*Andrew Sassoli-Walker*)

Right: Aurora's colourfully lit name competes with a near-midnight Norwegian sunset. (*Bob Walker*)

AURORA

I had the privilege of being the Managing Director of P&O Cruises during the development of *Oriana*, originally conceived to replace the venerable *Canberra*. As the time for *Oriana*'s entry into service approached it was realised that interest was so high both vessels could be operated alongside each other and *Canberra* remained in service.

Many loyal passengers travelled on *Oriana* in her first year but missed the traditional nature of *Canberra* and returned to her the following season. Although *Canberra* had an unbelievable degree of passenger loyalty her age was then more noticeable in comparison with the modern facilities available on her new sibling. As a steamship she was expensive to operate and increasing maintenance bills could not be afforded. So, in 1996, the decision was finally made to retire *Canberra* the following year and a search for a replacement commenced – for the second time.

Initially another vessel from the worldwide fleet was transferred to the UK and renamed *Arcadia* (the third P&O vessel so called). However, the interest being generated by the introduction of our new vessels was creating extraordinary demand so a further ship was contracted to be built at Meyer Werft, the builder of *Oriana*. Some key negotiations relating to this contract were held on the day of a commemorative dinner on board *Canberra* marking the fifteenth anniversary of the Falklands campaign, an event attended by the former Prime Minister, Margaret Thatcher, and many other dignitaries. This was the last event of its kind held on board *Canberra* but my attention was more on my phone as discussions went on through the night with Meyer Werft in Germany.

The following morning agreement was reached to build *Aurora*, a vessel designed very much with the future in mind and representing a distinct break with the past. Aimed at a younger clientele, the concept was to appeal to those who wanted a modern interpretation of British cruising suitable for the twenty-first century. Whilst the team of design architects and technical staff were largely the same as those who developed *Oriana*, their brief reflected this change in approach.

Another difference was that whilst *Oriana* had been built directly for the British flag, *Aurora* was quite unique in being supervised by the Liberian authorities, whose base was in the USA. On completion of the build the Liberian flag was raised – very briefly – before being replaced by the Red Ensign. Such are the consequences of arcane maritime regulation!

On arrival in Southampton *Aurora* was named by the Princess Royal but, to the consternation of everyone present, the Champagne bottle used for the naming failed to break on hitting the bow, an event reputed to bring bad luck. A day later a quiet renaming ceremony was held, undertaken by a crew member by the name of Aurora, and a bottle was successfully broken. This did not prevent a technical malfunction on the first night of the maiden voyage, which caused its curtailment and massive media interest. Once resolved *Aurora* went into service and became equally successful as her illustrious predecessors.

Gwyn Hughes
Managing Director, P&O Cruises 1983–2003

Chapter 1

THE PENINSULAR & ORIENTAL STEAM NAVIGATION COMPANY TO P&O CRUISES

In the days of the British Empire and increasing colonial expansion, the ships of the Peninsular & Oriental Steam Navigation Company offered a lifeline to families spread all over the globe – a floating bridge as it was called at the time. The company came to represent reliability, service and tradition. The story began in 1815 when Brodie McGhie Willcox opened an office in London as a ship broker. He employed a clerk, Arthur Anderson, who had grown up in the Shetland Islands and served in the Royal Navy. In 1822, Willcox offered Anderson a partnership and they set up their first business together, running cargo between Falmouth in Cornwall and the Iberian Peninsula.

However, both men held a passionate belief in the possibilities offered by the new steamships. With financial backing from a Dublin ship owner, Capt. Richard Bourne, they founded The Peninsular Steam Navigation Company, operating with just one wooden paddle-steamer, *William Fawcett*. They soon had sufficient business for a second steamer, *Royal Tar,* and together, these ships became the first of what eventually grew into a mighty fleet, known and admired all over the world.

Initially they ran at a loss, but kept faith with their belief in offering more capacity than the market then required, believing if the service was there, the business would follow. What they needed for financial stability was a Government mail contract. At that time the delivery of overseas mail was the responsibility of the Admiralty. Most of this was still sent by sailing vessel and the service was slow and irregular. In contrast, Willcox and Anderson guaranteed to deliver mail from Falmouth to Lisbon at cheaper cost, greater speed and on a regular schedule. Following commercial pressure, the Government invited tenders to operate a steamship mail service between the UK and Alexandria in Egypt. On 22 August 1837, they formally signed a contract with The Peninsular Steam Navigation Company, who were the lowest bidders. This was one of the first private mail contracts in the world. Had it not been a success it is possible that the North Atlantic service (among others), which later put Samuel Cunard on the way to fame and fortune, may not have been similarly opened to tender..

In 1840, the Government invited tenders for a similar steam packet service between Suez and India. Once again Willcox and Anderson supplied the lowest bid and in December 1840 the company was formally incorporated by Royal Charter. In recognition of their new routes, Oriental was added to the company's name, which was swiftly shortened to, and known all over the world as, P&O. On 1 September the company's new 1,800 ton steamship *Oriental* left for Alexandria on the first extended sailing. The mail and passengers would then travel overland to Suez and onwards to Calcutta in ships of the East India Company, working in co-operation with P&O.

Opposite: Arthur Anderson is commemorated on board *Oriana* and *Aurora* in the name of a bar, the décor reminiscent of a traditional Gentleman's Club. (*Andrew Sassoli-Walker*)

This page: A fine half-model of *Strathnaver* is mounted in the Crow's Nest bar on *Aurora*. (*Andrew Sassoli-Walker*)

The highly polished bell on *Canberra*, with her distinctive twin funnels in the background. (*Andrew Sassoli-Walker*)

The P&O Cruises house flag on the jack staff of *Oriana* hangs limply in the heat of Arrecife, Lanzarote, while underneath the bow is the traditional rising sun logo of P&O Cruises. (*Andrew Sassoli-Walker*)

In 1844, the satirist and writer William Thackeray spent a couple of months sailing around the Mediterranean, compliments of P&O. It was not a cruise in the modern sense, since his journey involved several overnight stays ashore and changes of vessel but the book he published on his return, *From Cornhill to Grand Cairo,* highlighted the pleasure that could be had from sea travel for its own sake. His writings provided free and valuable publicity for P&O and, in a twist to the saying that the sun never set on the British Empire, he wrote that, 'The sun never sets on a P&O ship.'

The following year P&O extended services beyond India to Singapore and China, adding Australia to their routes seven years later. In 1854, the company also took over the Suez to Bombay route when the East India Company's power reverted to the Crown. Up until 1872 virtually all communication between the UK and India, China, Japan and Australia was in the hands of P&O, who then owned the largest commercial fleet of steamships in the world, and it is easy to see how they developed an almost mythological status unique in history. In nearly five hundred journeys to Melbourne, Australia, only seven were more than one hour late arriving!

Like Thackeray many years earlier, some people were using the main liner routes, combined with those of the branch line vessels, as a way of seeing the world. In 1904, P&O capitalised on this trend and introduced their first cruise ship to the fleet by converting the liner *Rome* (1881–1904) into a 'cruising yacht', renaming her *Vectis* (1904–12). These proved so popular that they soon introduced a much larger vessel, the 11,000 ton *Mantua.*

Following the severe losses of shipping in the First World War, P&O set about an expansive rebuilding programme. They ordered twenty ships to be delivered between 1920 and 1938 including a series of five liners for the Australian service, known as the *Strath* class – *Stratheden, Strathmore, Strathnaver, Strathaird* and *Strathallan* – the first company ships to be designed from the start for cruising as well as line voyages. These were the first of the large express liners to carry the livery well-known today. At just over 22,000 tons, the white hulls and buff funnels made them an imposing sight and gained them the nickname the 'White Sisters'.

P&O Cruises has come a very long way since those early days of cruising. Their last liner was *Canberra* (1961–1997), built to carry emigrants to Australia – including the famous £10 Poms. However, it was not long before the introduction of the Boeing 747 and other wide-bodied, long-haul airliners brought an end to line voyages to P&O's long-standing destinations. Conversely, cruising was growing in popularity and *Canberra* gained a new lease of life when she was converted into a single-class cruise ship in the 1970s.

The first ship designed and built for P&O's Princess brand was *Royal Princess* in 1984, but she was planned for the US market and after her naming ceremony left Southampton for Los Angeles, which became her home port for the next few years. It was not until the launch of *Oriana* in 1995 that UK passengers finally had their own purpose-built cruise ship. *Aurora* followed five years later and since then P&O Cruises has built three more new vessels with *Arcadia, Ventura* and *Azura,* the latter two each carrying over 3,000 passengers. With *Oceana* (ex *Ocean Princess*) and the boutique-sized *Adonia* (ex *Royal Princess [2]*), the cruising fleet is the largest it has ever been. Trends suggest that the cruise market will continue to grow, albeit more slowly than the last few years, and P&O Cruises is planning to add an eighth ship to the fleet in 2015. At 141,000 tonnes, this will be their largest vessel yet and is an indication of their commitment to the British market

Chapter 2

PROJECT GEMINI – THE £200M GAMBLE

P&O Cruises began to consider building a new ship to replace the aging but much-loved *Canberra* as far back as 1988. The cruising market was then very different from that of today. The number of British choosing to cruise was growing slowly but the Caribbean had become the most popular destination and the majority of new vessels were designed for that part of the world – ships such as Holland America Line's *Westerdam* and Royal Caribbean's *Sovereign of the Seas*.

If you wanted to sail from the UK you were limited to very few ships, among them P&O Cruises' *Canberra*, Cunard's *Queen Elizabeth 2*, Fred Olsen's *Black Prince* and Charter Cruise Club's (CTC) Russian ships. During the summer some American ships, including *Pacific Princess* (one of the original Love Boats from the popular television series) and Norwegian America Line's *Vistafjord* and *Sagafjord*, began to appear on the scene as US passengers began to discover a taste for visiting the Old World. These cruises were also on sale to British passengers and began to grow in popularity. However, the figures for ex-UK cruising were not looking that promising. Although 1987 saw an annual increase of 10,500 passengers, bringing the total to 51,500, the numbers decreased slightly the following year and fell even further in 1990 to 47,000. Despite this downward trend, P&O Cruises forecast that the growing popularity of cruising in general would see the UK market follow, given time.

However, even after the new ship was finally ordered in 1991, and with an upward trend again in the numbers of people cruising, many sceptics assumed she would be a direct replacement for *Canberra*. In fact P&O Cruises had by then discarded this idea, believing there would be sufficient business to risk operating both ships out of Southampton, while *Sea Princess,* which had returned to ex-UK cruising from a period in Australia, would be sent to operate fly-cruises based in the Mediterranean.

The investment by P&O Cruises to spend £200 million on a ship for the UK market was seen by some as a huge gamble. At the time, David Dingle, then P&O Cruises' Marketing Director (now CEO of Carnival UK) was quoted as saying, 'Any large and successful cruise line should always have

Opposite: *Canberra*, dressed overall at 38/39 berth at the Queen Elizabeth II Terminal Southampton in the twilight of her illustrious career. (*Andrew Sassoli-Walker*)

Above: Old meets new – *Oriana*, bathed in sunshine at 43/4 berth two days after her naming ceremony, while *Canberra* embarks passengers for another cruise, 8 April 1995. (*Andrew Sassoli-Walker*)

Right: Second Officer Lindsay Petrie with the Golden Cockerel on the bridge wing of *Oriana*. This symbol is awarded to the fastest ship in the P&O fleet. On *Canberra*'s final cruise in 1997 it was handed over to *Oriana* when both ships were anchored off Cannes. Boats were sent out to perform the handover. Before *Canberra*, it was held by the previous *Oriana* (1960–1986). (*Sharon Poole*)

Computer-aided artist's impression of Project Gemini – the first image released when the new ship was announced. (P&O Cruises)

plans for new ships available'. He continued, 'Opportunities to order new ships vary enormously according to exchange rates, shipyard availability, and the financial packages on offer at any particular time. Companies must be ready to take advantage of any window of opportunity.'

Project Gemini was born of the discussions which took place over many years from 1988. The new ship had to be stronger and faster than vessels that operated solely in the relatively calm conditions of the Caribbean. Passengers want to get to the sun quickly, so it had to be capable of operational speeds of up to 24 knots. This would allow varied itineraries within the average fourteen day cruise. Incidentally, *Oriana* still holds the Golden Cockerel traditionally awarded to the fastest ship in the P&O Cruises fleet. Previous holders include *Canberra* and the first *Oriana*. Additionally, this fast speed had to be maintained in the potentially unpredictable Bay of Biscay, which has to be crossed when heading to destinations south from P&O Cruises' home port of Southampton.

To win over both new and existing passengers, the design of the new ship had to reflect the best of *Canberra*, while introducing new facilities and technology throughout. It had to have the fuel, fresh water and stores capacity to operate world-wide itineraries and be able to transit through the Panama and Suez Canals. This last requirement dictated a maximum beam of 32 metres. Above all, she had to appeal to and capture no less than 10 per cent of the UK cruise market (including those die-hard *Canberra* passengers) to be viable, unlike US ships which only needed 2 per cent of their much larger passenger base. To this end a wide variety of cabin types and fares were essential. P&O Cruises' Project Gemini evolved to incorporate all these requirements so that as soon as conditions were right to place an order, the company could move quickly. As there was no existing reference ship, it was essentially a plan for a concept vessel.

Having reached this stage, the project was handed over to P&O subsidiary Three Quays Marine Services, to produce the General Arrangement Plans which were to be used to invite tenders from selected shipyards. The initial quotes were well over P&O Cruises' budget and the whole project was temporarily shelved. Six months later it was reviewed and it was decided that the ship could be reduced in size and still comfortably hold the same number of passengers. Two of the original ten shortlisted ships' yards were asked to re-quote on the revised design. *Oriana* was about to become a reality.

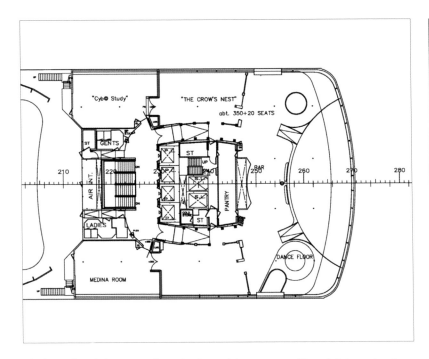

Clockwise from left: Extract from the General Arrangement Plan of *Oriana*, showing the Crow's Nest bar. It was designed on two levels so as many people as possible could have a view through the floor-to-ceiling windows. (Carnival UK)

The Crow's Nest bar on *Canberra*. This venue was one of the popular features carried forward into the design of *Oriana* (*Andrew Sassoli-Walker*)

The Crow's Nest bar on *Oriana* was heavily influenced by the similar popular venue on *Canberra*. (*Patrick Sutcliffe*)

Chapter 3

REALISING THE DREAM - THE DESIGN & BUILDING OF *ORIANA*

Historically, all P&O Cruises' ships had been built in the United Kingdom and the few yards still operating were among the ten shipbuilders originally approached by P&O Cruises to tender for the new vessel. In the event none of the UK yards were interested in, or capable of, tendering and out of the final two firms shortlisted, the order went to Meyer Werft of Germany who came up with the best combination of price, design and delivery date. This was not a decision welcomed by the press, who were critical of the fact the ship was not to be built in the UK, but who had little understanding of the reasons why.

Meyer Werft had been building ships for over 200 years from their yards in Papenburg, some 45 km (30 miles) up the River Ems in Lower Saxony. Papenburg was once a major centre for ship building with over thirty yards based along the river, although by 1995 this had dwindled to just one – Meyer Werft. At the time *Oriana* was ordered, the company owned the largest indoor construction dock in the world – big enough to fit the Houses of Parliament inside!

Much of the early work on the new vessel – then known by her shipyard No. 636 – had been undertaken by Meyer Werft staff long before any formal contract had been signed. Once it was agreed, they brought in teams of specialist designers for different areas of the ship – public rooms, cabins and so on. This design team was led by the Swedish marine architect Robert Tillberg, whom P&O Cruises had brought in originally to rough out specifications for the tendering documents. Tillberg was a true pioneer in ship design, often questioning prevailing 'truths' to produce innovative designs. For example it was Tillberg who designed the very first modern-style atrium on a ship – *Sea Venture* – in 1969. When he presented the idea to the engineers at Rheistahl Nordseewerke, they laughed, telling him it was impossible to build a ship with a big hole in the middle. Tillberg quietly pointed out that oil tankers have a big hole in the middle too!

Meyer Werft precisely summed up the ship when they said that, 'The underlying idea behind *Oriana* is to combine state-of-the-art technology in navigation, consumer electronics and on-board hotel management with the comfort and time-honoured British style of an ocean liner.'

Charles Arkinstall, then Director of Fleet Services at P&O and Princess Cruises, recalls, 'P&O Cruises had a very clear idea of what they wanted so we spent a lot of time pre-contract in getting the general arrangement and specification right. *Oriana* was a something of a step change for Meyer Werft at the time as they had built only three cruise ships (*Homeric*, *Crown Odyssey* and *Horizon*) and were close to finishing their fourth (*Zenith*) when we placed the order. At the time, we had jointly developed a very detailed specification, a general arrangement and all the other usual drawings but additionally had had Robert Tillberg produce basic drawings for all public areas to define the standard required and to show some of the detailing as we really didn't have a suitable reference ship. As a result of this pre-contractual effort [Project Gemini], the arrangement of *Oriana* as delivered was very similar to that agreed at the time of contract with few changes of any substance.'

Once the contract was officially signed in December 1991, detailed specifications were drawn up – very detailed in fact – there were twenty-two pages on paint application alone! Marine engineer and ex-Royal Navy captain Jim Hunter was contracted as overall project manager. He described this extremely complicated task. 'At the beginning of each project, the team for both *Oriana* and *Aurora* was quite small and consisted of a chief engineer, a purser and myself. It sat, rather like a cuckoo in the nest of the Newbuild Team at Southampton, vying for the attention of the specialists who made up the rest of Newbuild and who were also engaged on other projects for Princess Cruises. In time, when the build started, the team swelled to include the site manager and inspectors, followed by the gradually increasing numbers of sea staff who would eventually take over the vessel at completion.'

'The easiest way to describe what the project team was about is to briefly describe its interfaces with other groups – essentially there were internal

The main bridge consoles on *Oriana*. (*Andrew Sassoli-Walker*)

and external interfaces. Of the internal faces the largest was with the rest of the Newbuild Team. About 10,000 documents (drawings, letters, etc.) per year pass through the project, fortunately electronically, and nearly all of these find their way to the specialists on whom the project relies for expertise. There was also an internal interface with every department in P&O Cruises for, increasingly as the build progresses, each department has a role to play. Initially their input assisted the design but then turned towards preparations for the introduction of the vessel into service. The final internal face is with the Directors. Keeping them informed on progress, seeking approval for architectural designs in the passenger areas, requesting approval of modifications to the build specification, and

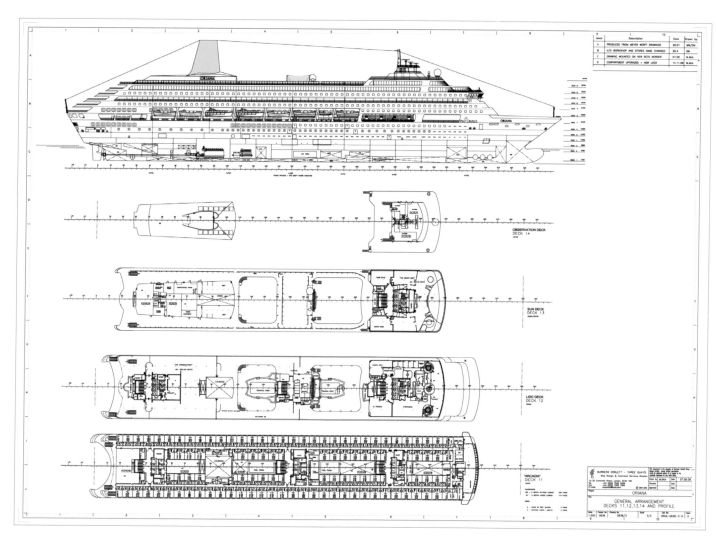

Part of the General Arrangement Plans of *Oriana* (Decks 11–14) before the present sponson or ducktail was fitted. (Carnival UK)

tweaking their tails if they didn't make decisions in time, were all part of this important interface.'

'Of the external interfaces, the largest was with the shipyard, and in particular with my opposite number, the Meyer Werft Project Manager. Both P&O Cruises and Meyer Werft had design responsibilities; the former for all passenger areas, galleys, pantries, laundries and entertainment systems, and the latter for the hull, machinery, crew areas, stores, navigation and safety. The result is an immense exchange of design and build information between the parties and accounts for the majority of the 10,000 documents per year mentioned above. While some documents were for information, the greater number was for approval by the other party.'

'Other external interfaces were with companies which undertook the interiors and for which P&O Cruises was responsible. Foremost amongst them was with the architects whose designs would eventually grace both ships. They were involved throughout the design and build phases, and 'managing' them was a special pleasure.'

'Overall the role of the Project Manager was to keep the show on the road, on time, to the expected quality and within budget. What did the Project Manager feel like? Like a windscreen wiper blade, endlessly sweeping across the project front-line to detect and prevent any small obstacles becoming big ones which could impede the planned advance!'

In addition, P&O Cruises set up a Technical Services Support Group (TSSG) in Southampton. This was headed up by Charles Arkinstall, and was responsible for all newbuild ships. He recalls, 'My colleagues and I spent several weeks in the autumn of 1991 in Papenburg developing the technical specification and principal drawings for *Oriana*. Our home base at the time was still Monaco [they relocated to Southampton in 1992], not the easiest place to get to and from Papenburg, and as we wanted to get the job finished, we spent the weekends working in Meyer's offices.

Marine engineer Richard Vie, currently Vice President of Technical & Quality Assurance at Carnival Corporate Shipbuilding, was Technical Services Manager for both *Oriana* and *Aurora*. He is pictured with a model of *Aurora* at Carnival House, Southampton, March 2012. (*Andrew Sassoli-Walker*)

Bernard and all his colleagues were most hospitable throughout and relationships were excellent, although given that the Queen was due to name the ship on a very specific day arranged a long time in advance, there were a few tensions towards the end.'

Marine engineer Richard Vie, currently Vice President of Technical & Quality Assurance at Carnival Corporate Shipbuilding, was an engineer working for Sitmar when the company was purchased by P&O. He was immediately transferred to the project team as Technical Services Manager.

The designers had a strict brief in that the ship had to appeal to the British cruise market and in particular those loyal *Canberra* passengers. To gain inspiration and to find out what it was about *Canberra* that worked (in a design sense), and indeed didn't work, Tillberg spent a lot of time on board, talking to passengers and crew. While US passengers like a floating hotel, the British want a ship to feel like a ship. This radically affected the design of *Oriana*, from the amount of deck space to the shape of the bow. For example, the angled lifeboat davits on *Oriana* were inspired by those on *Canberra* and even *Oriana*'s funnel is designed to bear some resemblance to *Canberra*'s twin stacks. P&O Cruises also wanted a shallow draft and slim ship, to maximise the number of ports at which she would be able to berth. Model tests of the proposed hull design were vital at this stage to test sea-keeping ability and hydrodynamics and these led to the bow being lengthened to improve these aspects. Charles Arkinstall again: '*Oriana*'s hull design had to be a balance between the true ocean liner such as *QE2*, and the more conventional cruise ship primarily operating in relatively benign conditions, mainly on account of her operational base, which for nine months of the year would be out of Southampton. Project Gemini adhered too closely to the concept of a liner and the numbers simply did not add up so we had to come up with a compromise – essentially a cruise liner able to cross Biscay mid-winter, with a higher speed capability (Southampton to the Eastern Mediterranean and back in 16 days with a minimum of 5 ports), and without losing too many cabins so as to meet the required rate of return on the investment, based on P&O Cruises' predicted revenues.

'*Oriana* doesn't have an extended bow *per se* but she does have a finer entry forward, without the pronounced shoulder to be seen on most 'conventional' cruise ships which allows cabins to be continued well forward close to the waterline. Consequently *Oriana* has slightly fewer cabins than a conventional cruise vessel of a similar size. She also had

heavier scantlings [structural longitudinal and transverse beams and bulkheads] given the expectation of less favourable weather, and of course her higher speed required a long optimisation process in the design of her hull and propellers.'

Unlike most American cruisers, many British passengers particularly enjoy sea days as well as port visits. Those two or three days down to the Mediterranean or Canary Islands allow people time to relax, get to know each other and enjoy time out on deck. There is plenty of outside space on *Oriana*, not only on her upper decks and stern, but also on her wrap-around promenade deck, all of which is surfaced with 2½ acres of solid teak, ethically sourced from a plantation. As Lord Sterling said, 'Cruise ships in the past always had a promenade deck so *Oriana* has one; if you cannot walk all the way round a ship, it's simply not the same.' He was also determined that the new ship would have a traditional tiered stern. This is still one of *Oriana*'s most distinctive and elegant features.

The man charged with fitting out her cabins and suites, Norwegian Petter Yran, based his colour schemes on warm tones highlighted with traditional marine-style brass fittings. In another move catering specifically for UK passengers, 50 per cent of cabins have a bath rather than the shower preferred by US travellers. *Oriana* was to have smaller public rooms than similar sized American ships, but more of them – seventeen in fact. These areas were designed by Scot John McNeece. Like Tillberg much of his previous experience had been designing ships for the US market, so some first-hand research was required - visiting pubs,

Opposite: *Oriana* doing what she was designed to do – speeding through the ocean taking passengers to the sun. (P&O Cruises)

Right: The Riviera Pool and funnel, *Oriana*. (Andrew Sassoli-Walker)

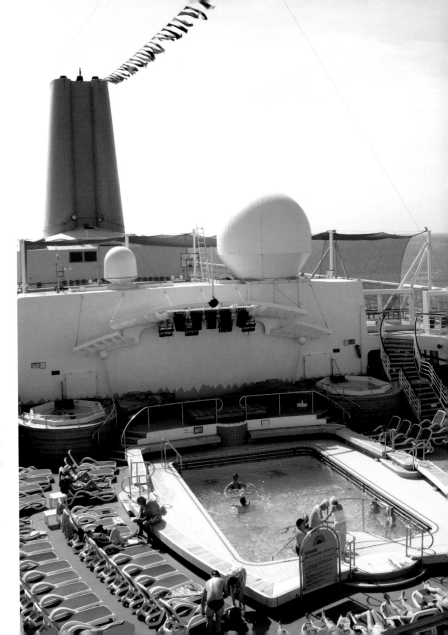

Left: Afternoon sunshine on the wide teak promenade deck of *Oriana*, as she sailed through the Mediterranean to Egypt, November 2005. (*Sharon Poole*)

Opposite left: The Pacific show lounge, *Oriana*. (*Andrew Sassoli-Walker*)

Opposite right: The Theatre Royal, *Oriana*. This was unique at the time for having completely unimpeded sight lines, as well as individual air-conditioning built into the back of every seat. (*Andrew Sassoli-Walker*)

shops and clubs throughout the UK. It was decided early on that *Oriana* should have a West End style theatre rather than a show lounge (although in fact she has both). The theatre was perhaps the most stunning, and technologically difficult room to construct. When *Oriana* entered service, it was the first sea-going theatre offering completely unimpaired sight lines from every seat. This caused a few headaches at the design stage and extra internal columns were added to the decks above and below to maintain integrity, as well as thicker steel being used around the theatre itself. Charles Arkinstall: 'The designers had been studying how to ensure the structural elements were, in so far as is possible and necessary, designed to suit the location rather than the location to suit the structure as was the norm in the past. Many spaces can accommodate pillars without problems but theatres are best without. Fortunately, above theatres are often to be found cabins at the sides and air conditioning spaces in the middle, and these lend themselves to being used to provide

a continuous steel girder between the bulkheads at each end of the theatre to support the theatre ceiling, and to pick up the loads from the pillars supporting the decks above and transfer this to the main bulkheads.'

The innovation did not stop on the audience's side of the curtain. There was a revolving stage with West End standard lighting controls, an orchestra pit which could be raised or lowered and, for the first time on a P&O Cruises' ship, performers had a proper dressing room. *Oriana's* Theatre Royal alone cost £1 million.

The keel for Hull No. 636 was laid on 11 March 1993 when a British penny and a German pfennig were laid under the first block, in an ancient ceremony dating from Viking times and believed to bring good luck to a ship. From that point on 2,000 men worked to complete the project in around two years. As with ship construction today, *Oriana* was assembled in a dry dock from forty-nine huge prefabricated steel sections, although the superstructure above deck twelve is aluminium to save weight.

Left: Lifting one of the prefabricated sections of *Oriana* into place in the building dock at Papenburg. (Meyer Werft)

Opposite: Oriana starts to take shape as each section is craned into position and welded together. As soon as each part is in place, fitting-out of that section can start, even though the hull is still incomplete. (Meyer Werft)

Each took a month to build in an assembly shop close by and was then hoisted into position by crane and welded in place. The largest block was No. 16 which weighed in at 722 tonnes and housed the main engines. In June 1994, the final block was fitted – the upper section of the bow. The advantage of this method of assembly is that the fitting out of each section can begin as soon as it is welded in place.

Jim Hunter tells an interesting story of how *Oriana*'s name may have been chosen. 'The ship was built by first constructing blocks and then bringing them together to form the vessel. This means that once the build contract is signed, the detailed design work starts, and the roadmap for that is largely decided by the order in which the building blocks are constructed. The design process can take eighteen to twenty months to complete, but the build starts much earlier, and the pressure is on the project team to keep the completed design well ahead of the build. When Meyer Werft reached the stage of cutting steel for the bow section, they asked if the ship's name could be made known; the reason being that to weld on letters during construction is easier than when it is part of the vessel. At that time the ship's name was not known within the Newbuild

Team at Southampton, and I sent the request on to our head office in London. To make the sure the request was clearly understood, I attached a side elevation of the bow section and added a ship's name. I chose *Oriana*, for no good reason other than on looking through the names of previous P&O Cruises ships, I liked the name. To my astonishment, back came the answer *Oriana*. To this day I have no idea whether that drawing influenced the decision.'

It was about this time that Lord Sterling approached Commodore Ian Gibb, then in command of *Canberra*, and asked him to become the first Master of *Oriana*. Commodore Gibb recalls, 'My first reaction, as I was but two years from compulsory retirement at sixty in 1996, was to suggest that I may be too old for such an appointment. He was however insistent that I had something to offer, and as I was well-known to *Canberra* passengers, could act as a form of continuity between old and new.' By joining the ship while still in the build stage, Commodore Gibb was also able to offer suggestions and changes as the ship took shape. 'Although I had known about Project Gemini through the internal grapevine whilst in command of *Canberra*, it wasn't until mid-1994 that I was officially approached to become captain of the new ship ... My promotion to Commodore of the joint P&O and Princess fleets had just come through on 9 August 1994, and after some shore leave in September and October, I paid my first visit to *Oriana* on 11 December 1994. I had unknowingly given a goodly amount of input during the early part of 1994 as the architect, Robert Tillberg, had travelled with us aboard *Canberra* on a fact-finding mission with a view to incorporating some of her design features in the new-build. In the event, in my view, he achieved an excellent compromise. My influence on the design was down to my rapport with Tillberg and I was able to, perhaps, draw his attention to design features which worked well, and probably more importantly to where, over the years, we had learned that improvements could be made.'

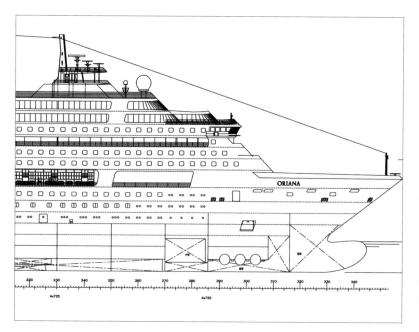

Far left: Part of the General Arrangement Plan showing *Oriana*'s bow. (Carnival UK)

Left: Commodore Ian Gibb, first master of *Oriana*. (*Commodore Ian Gibb*)

Opposite top: Capt. Hamish Reid with a pilot on the bridge wing of *Oriana* as they prepare to depart from Funchal, Madeira, November 2007. (*Andrew Sassoli-Walker*)

Opposite bottom: Starboard bridge wing, *Oriana*. The original plans called for an enclosed bridge wing but Commodore Gibb preferred to judge the wind by feel and so the design was altered at his request. (*Andrew Sassoli-Walker*)

One area of difference was over whether to build the ship with open or enclosed bridge wings. The design called for enclosed wings, not least to protect the delicate electronics. Commodore Gibb was one of several people consulted over this matter and as he put it, 'I was looked upon as a "dinosaur" in my wish to have the open version. I always liked to have the feel of the wind on my face – a view shared by many of the senior pilots around the world – and having been, at this stage, over forty years at sea, the importance of a sense of feel had been drummed into me by my mentors over the years. In any event, the electronic wind indicators that were fitted frequently provided duff information, as the base instrument was mounted up the mast and was periodically in a blind spot as regards information collection – updraught, downdraught, etc. The direction vane quite often revolved at speed with no indication of the relative direction. To obviate any misunderstanding I had the stern jack hoisted on approaching a berth to give an indication of wind strength. And so ... I got wet and windswept, but always achieved safe dockings! My greatest supporter in this battle was Jeffrey Sterling himself who ensured that my wishes were incorporated into the design. I had always been influenced by the loss of the New Zealand ferry *Wahine* in Wellington Harbour as the ship was one of the first to have enclosed bridge wings and the Enquiry found that the master had not fully appreciated the danger and strength of the wind by being indoors.' Another change that Commodore Gibb made to the bridge was to insist on having a traditional ship's steering wheel in addition to the modern joystick control (nicknamed the 'Lipstick' due to its manufacturer, Lips of The Netherlands). 'I like to have a back-up', he commented.

Commodore Gibb joined a well-established group of senior officers already based in Papenburg to supervise the new-build. This included Chief Engineer Marcus (Mark) James and Chief Officer Hamish Reid (most recently master of *Oriana*, now retired). Between them they were able to select the remainder of *Oriana*'s crew as well as influence particular design features they felt were important to the smooth running of the ship. As with any vessel, it is the people that really make her what she is and their selection of staff created the perfect transition for nervous or doubting ex-*Canberra* passengers.

Hamish Reid recalled his sixteen months in Papenburg. His task was to liaise with the building team and shipyard to ensure they got all that was specified regarding the bridge, safety and deck areas. He continued, 'During my time there I was working out how we would operate the vessel and what training requirements we would have for the officers and crew allocated to the ship. I also worked with the other departmental disciplines to produce a ship able to go to work as soon as she was ready for service.' The three senior deck officers all practised handling *Oriana* using specialist simulators. Commodore Gibb recalled that not once did they manage to berth her, always ending up in the car park – fortunately an event that didn't occur with the real vessel! *Oriana* was the first fly-by-wire ship and the Integrated Bridge System was a good five years ahead of its time, leading the way for all future cruise ship control systems. One single console covered command, navigation and communication controls. Screens showed the current speed as well as that required to reach the next port on time; track pilot and speed

This page: Crowds gather in the late afternoon sunshine to see *Oriana* depart after her first visit to La Coruña, Spain, 1 August 1996. Commodore Gibb and the staff captain watch them from the port bridge wing. (*Michael Whittingham*)

Oriana's bridge controls, with a conventional semi-wooden ship's wheel in the centre console. (*Andrew Sassoli-Walker*)

The Lips joystick control on *Oriana*, aptly nicknamed the lipstick! This is used to control all movement – forward, sideways and reverse. (*Andrew Sassoli-Walker*)

pilot were all automated. Once a destination and time were input, in theory, the ship could navigate itself without human input, although that was never going to happen. Richard Vie recalled the time when Commodore Gibb realised that Siemens could dial into the ship and take remote control of their equipment and systems for maintenance and monitoring. He was only reassured that it wouldn't happen at sea when it was suggested he could always unplug the modem line!

While built in Germany, components for *Oriana* were sourced from all over the world, although UK firms were chosen wherever possible. The stabilisers, for example, were built by Brown Brothers of Edinburgh and at the time were the largest ever fitted to a ship. Each fin with its associated housing and equipment weighed 187 tons. The fins are 7.5 metres long and are operated by a computer that senses the roll of the vessel. They

Far left: The Integrated Bridge System on *Oriana*, with screens for track pilot, radar, etc., with engine and other controls situated within convenient reach of the captain's chair. (*Sharon Poole*)

Left: Oriana's air-conditioning plant built by Grenco. It was the first time that units this large had been built for use on a ship, and they had to be delivered to Papenburg in two pieces due to their size. (The Ship's Photographer)

can work to a maximum of 21.5 degrees up or down and at 18 knots have a 90 per cent roll reduction. The air conditioning units were also manufactured in the UK by Grenco. Air conditioning is one of the prime users of electrical power on a ship and in tropical waters can take up to 60 per cent of the ship's electrical load.

The eight four-stroke diesel engines were made by MAN B&W in Germany and are arranged in pairs of a nine-cylinder and a six-cylinder with the smaller engine outboard of the larger one. This arrangement is known as 'father & son' configuration. Four engines are used for propulsion and four as auxiliaries to provide mains power on board. One of *Oriana's* auxiliary engines can produce sufficient power for a town of up to 50,000 people!

The twin propellers were controllable-pitch, the blades made from melted down coins, made obsolete by the opening up of Eastern Europe.

Three bow thrusters and one stern thruster were fitted, all manufactured by Lips of The Netherlands. Like the propellers, they are controllable-pitch so that each is able to thrust from port to starboard and vice versa without changing the direction of rotation.

In April 1994, Lord Sterling flew out to Papenburg to view progress. The interior design was constantly under review and on this visit he felt the ceiling height of one of the restaurants was too low, and so at no small cost, it was increased. In the later stages, the project team tried to discourage Lord Sterling from visiting until all the snagging had been completed as he was such a perfectionist. Jim Hunter: 'It was during the final stages of *Oriana's* build that Lord Sterling made a number of visits to tour the vessel. On one occasion it was almost midnight by the time we reached the Crow's Nest which was by now fully furnished but

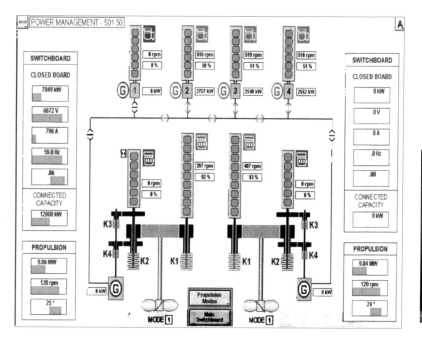

Far left: Computer diagram of the power management system for *Oriana's* father and son engine configuration. (*David Jewkes*)

Left: Oriana's three starboard controllable-pitch bow thrusters, made, like her propellers, by Lips of The Netherlands. (The Ship's Photographer)

the room lighting did not meet Lord Sterling's approval, and despite many adjustments to the various lighting dimmer switches, the results remained unsatisfactory. This was noted down and changes made before his next visit.'

Hull No. 636 was floated out into the hot sunshine of the Papenburg Basin on 15 July 1994 and taken to the fitting-out berth for final completion. As she was reversed out of the building dock, her funnel was lifted into place and she appeared in her final form for the first time. *Oriana's* first voyage was the 45 km transit down the River Ems from Papenburg to the port of Emden at the mouth of the river. At the best of times this journey is difficult and *Oriana*

was the largest passenger ship to be built in Germany since 1914. There are sections of shallow water and the river has to be constantly dredged to keep the main channel clear. A railway bridge had to be dismantled for her to pass and overhead electricity cables tightened to clear the funnel. The first problem soon became apparent when it was realised *Oriana* was riding deeper in the water than expected, mainly due to the high quality, and therefore weightier, steel used in her construction. The ship was laden to the barest minimum regarding both equipment and personnel. Even the tenders and lifeboats were removed. These were all motored down the river separately, the whole procession resembling a mother duck with her brood of ducklings!

This page: The Oriental Restaurant, *Oriana.* Having windows on all three sides was a revelation to passengers used to Canberra's inside dining room. (*Andrew Sassoli-Walker*)

The attention to detail on *Oriana* even went so far as the customised fabric on the chairs in the Crow's Nest. (*Andrew Sassoli-Walker*)

The piano in the Crow's Nest on *Oriana,* which Lord Sterling originally felt was too small for the space. (*Sharon Poole*)

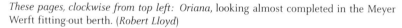

These pages, clockwise from top left: Oriana, looking almost completed in the Meyer Werft fitting-out berth. (*Robert Lloyd*)

The hand-over ceremony for *Oriana* with, from left to right, Tim Harris, Chairman of P&O Cruises, Bernard Meyer of Meyer Werft and master of *Oriana*, Commodore Ian Gibb. (*Michael Whittingham*)

Oriana was going to be larger in gross registered tons than Cunard's *Queen Elizabeth 2* (both ships pictured here at Southampton). Whether coincidence or a deliberate move on the part of Cunard, *QE2* underwent a refit shortly after *Oriana*'s launch, which increased internal passenger space and so retaining her title of Britain's largest passenger ship. (*Andrew Sassoli-Walker*)

Oriana, in the River Ems on her way to the sea for trials. She is not carrying her tenders and lifeboats at this stage, to reduce weight and consequently draught in the shallow river. Even with the reduction in weight, the Ems had to be dredged prior to *Oriana*'s transit. (*Robert Lloyd*)

Previous pages, from left: Oriana arrives at Southampton to a fireboat salute and crowds of well-wishers on Town Quay. (*Southern Daily Echo*)

Oriana arrives at Southampton, two days later than scheduled due to the problems that required dry docking. She was met by fire tugs but as it was now a weekday, a smaller than expected flotilla of welcoming craft. (*Carola Ingall*)

Oriana berthing at Southampton for the first time, as the P&O helicopter takes off after filming her arrival. (*Andrew Sassoli-Walker*)

Oriana comes alongside Berth 106, the Mayflower Cruise Terminal for the first time at Southampton, April 1995. (*John Peterson*)

At this stage Hull No. 636 was still under the command of the Meyer Werft yard team and the P&O Cruises team were there purely as observers. These builder's trials were to test out the navigation equipment and engines, with speed, turning and manoeuvring trials among much else. In the event they were most memorable for the atrocious weather that was encountered in the North Sea. Wherever the ship sailed, whether off Norway, Germany or Sweden, the winds never dropped below Force 7 and for much of the time were around Force 10–11. What they proved were the excellent sea-keeping abilities of the ship. However, a serious problem was noticed with vibration, caused by cavitation around the propellers. It was initially thought the propellers had touched the bed of the River Ems while transiting from the shipyard to the sea but this was not the case. *Oriana* was dry-docked in Hamburg between sea trials while solutions were sought. Finally, just four days before the naming ceremony, P&O Cruises agreed to formally accept the new ship – she came with a year's guarantee after all, but perhaps more importantly, there was an appointment with HM Queen Elizabeth II to keep! Back in Emden, at a ceremony watched by the whole ship's company assembled on the aft terraces, the German flag was struck and the Red Ensign raised for the first time. The ship's papers were handed over by Bernard Meyer to Tim Harris, Chairman of P&O Cruises and *Oriana* finally set sail under the command of P&O officers and crew.

On a hazy day in April 1995, the city of Southampton was alive with anticipation and excitement as *Oriana* sailed, a few days later than originally planned, into what was to become her new home port. The journey from Emden in Holland had been dogged with horrendous weather yet again.

Andrew Sassoli-Walker takes up the story. 'John Peterson, then P&O Containers' Port Agent at Tilbury, and I met up to watch *Oriana* arrive. With every maiden arrival or sailing of a cruise ship, there is an air of anticipation and atmosphere that is hard to describe. Both of us had sailed on *Canberra*, and working as we did within the P&O Group, albeit not with P&O Cruises, this was quite a significant moment. The crowds were already gathering as I dropped John off to board a pleasure boat going out to meet the vessel, and I chose a position at Dock Head, where the rivers Test and Itchen meet. It was not long before *Oriana* entered Southampton Water from the Solent. As she sailed towards her new home, she was saluted by the various vessels she passed, while the P&O Aviation helicopter circled overhead. As *Oriana* was arriving a couple of days later than planned and it was now a weekday rather than the weekend, the flotilla of small craft that would normally have been out to greet and escort her in was smaller than it might have been. As she approached Dock Head, the City of Southampton heard her deep whistle for the first time – she was home.'

Chapter 4

NAMING AND MAIDEN VOYAGE OF *ORIANA*

...And see! She stirs!
She starts, – she moves, – she seems to feel
The thrill of life along her keel,
And, spurning with her foot the ground,
With one exulting, joyous bound,
She leaps into the ocean's arms!
And lo! From the assembled crowd
There rose a shout, prolonged and loud,
That to the ocean seemed to say, –
"Take her, O bridegroom, old and grey,
Take her to thy protecting arms,
With all her youth and all her charms!"
The Building of the Ship by Henry W. Longfellow

Above left: Postcard of *Oriana* (1960–1986), sent from Honolulu in 1968. (*Sharon Poole collection*)

Above right: Capt. Hamish Reid beside the plaque from the *Oriana* (1960–1986), retrieved from storage and mounted in the Captain's Lounge on the new vessel. (*Sharon Poole*)

Oriana is the second ship to carry the name, which means Golden One in Latin. In the sixteenth century the name was often used in poetry and song to refer to Queen Elizabeth I and madrigals often ended with the words 'Long Live Fair Oriana'. The vessel was so called in honour of her predecessor SS *Oriana*, which served Orient Line and P&O from 1960 to 1986. To keep the memory of the old *Oriana* alive, P&O Cruises won a lengthy campaign to be able to allocate her radio call sign of GVSN to the new ship. Additionally, the double-E emblem that was mounted on the wall of the D-Deck foyer on the SS *Oriana* was retrieved from storage, refurbished at the expense of the crew of the older ship and mounted in the captain's lounge on the new vessel.

Oriana spent her first couple of days at the Mayflower Cruise Terminal while completing her provisioning and undertaking crew inductions. The commissioning purser was Chris Bullen and it was he who was responsible for ensuring the ship had everything required for the hotel operations side for both passengers and crew. This included making sure that all the new crew uniforms were fitted to the individuals that would be wearing them. To coincide with the launch of *Oriana* it was decided to introduce a new range of uniforms for all staff across the whole fleet.

A series of special events had been planned to introduce the ship to travel agents and members of P&O Cruises' loyalty club – the POSH Club, but her late arrival forced these to be compressed into just two days. Even so, some 10,000 visitors were able to have a preview of the new vessel. *Oriana* was moved to 43/4 berth the day before the naming ceremony. This berth was the site of the original Ocean Terminal from where the famous Cunard Queens sailed, along with other well-known transatlantic liners, and was directly opposite what is now the new Ocean Terminal. It was also from this berth that *Titanic* set sail in 1912 on her ill-fated maiden voyage to New York. Two Gala Evenings were held for VIPs and distinguished guests, with menus compiled by Swiss chef and restaurateur Anton Mosimann. While the guests were dining, the intention had been to cruise around the Isle of Wight. However, it had taken considerable skill to position *Oriana* to within an inch of the fixed gangways and, with heavy fog forecast, Commodore Gibb felt it would be imprudent to sail and risk not being able to berth her so precisely on their return, bearing in mind the darkness and probable impaired visibility.

Many of the guests stayed on board overnight and as dawn broke on 6 April 1995, the day began with a concert in the Crow's Nest lounge, hosted by radio and TV personality Richard Baker. This was followed by a classical piano recital by Dame Moura Lympany in the Pacific Lounge, accompanied by the Bernini Ensemble. Then the 2,500 guests assembled outside for the main event. HM Queen Elizabeth II arrived at Southampton at a temporary railway station set up on the dockside, where she was met by the Lord Lieutenant of Hampshire, Dame Mary Fagan. As the Choir of Westminster Abbey sang 'Fair Oriana, Beauty's Queen', HM the Queen, accompanied by HRH the Duke of Edinburgh, mounted the podium. Master of Ceremonies Leonard Pearcey opened proceedings by introducing the Royal Marine Band who then played an unusual rendition of 'Australian Sunrise' (complete with didgeridoo), in honour of the first *Oriana* and P&O's strong links with Australia. After speeches from Sir Keith Stuart, Chairman of Associated British Ports and Lord Sterling, Chairman of P&O, the Bishop of Basingstoke, the Rt Revd Dr Geoffrey Powell said prayers for the ship, her crew and future passengers, after which the Queen rose for the naming itself. After a short speech, including the time-honoured words, 'I name this ship *Oriana*, may God bless her and all who sail in her', the Queen pulled the lever to release the traditional bottle of Champagne which duly smashed against the bow. This was only the fourth merchant ship named by Her Majesty in her then forty-three year reign. The band struck up with the 'Skye Boat Song' ('Speed Bonny Boat') as the Royal Standard was broken out on the mast and the Queen boarded for a tour of the new vessel. Lunch was served to the Queen and other VIP guests, followed by a small ceremony in the Crichton Room at which she was presented with a silver model of *Oriana*. The Queen was also presented with a floral bouquet by Oriana Kelly, who had written to P&O Cruises as soon as she heard the name of the new ship. The final ceremony was the presentation of a sword by Lord Sterling to Commodore Gibb, in traditional naval recognition of a royal visit to a ship. The wives and partners of the VIPs also received a gift from P&O Cruises in the form of a blue and white Italian silk scarf designed by Caroline Charles and printed with images of most of the P&O passenger fleet from 1837 to the new *Oriana*. In 1992, Caroline Charles had been selected to design the official scarf to mark the fortieth anniversary of the accession of the Queen to the throne.

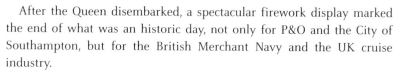

After the Queen disembarked, a spectacular firework display marked the end of what was an historic day, not only for P&O and the City of Southampton, but for the British Merchant Navy and the UK cruise industry.

Three days later, amid a gale of coloured streamers thrown from the promenade deck, and with a brass band playing on the quayside, *Oriana* set sail on her maiden voyage – a fourteen night cruise to the Canary Islands leaving Southampton on 9 April 1995, calling at Madeira, Tenerife, Lanzarote, Casablanca, Gibraltar, Praia da Rocha and Lisbon. Thousands of people lined the river banks from Mayflower Park to Calshot to watch the beautiful white ship sail past, preceded by fireboats and accompanied by an entourage of small craft to send her on her way.

It was Commodore Gibb's first maiden voyage as a master and no less memorable because of that. He commented towards the end of the cruise that, 'It has all gone better than we could have hoped. So much could have gone wrong, especially with the preparations having been so compressed at the end [due to *Oriana*'s late arrival in Southampton] – but it has been a triumph!'

Before departure, having gone to bed early, he received a phone call from the Reservations Department with what they called bad news! Lindi St Clair –otherwise known as Miss Whiplash, Britain's most famous twentieth century prostitute and political campaigner of the 1990s – was booked on the maiden voyage. Worse news – she was in a cabin next to Commodore Gibb! With memories of her outrageous behaviour on a previous *Canberra* cruise, which drew completely the kind of attention P&O Cruises could do without on their new flagship, on boarding, she was taken aside and sternly told to behave herself or she would be put off the ship there and then!

Opposite, from top left: View of the naming ceremony site at 43/4 berth from *Oriana*'s promenade deck with *Canberra* in the distance. A wall of brand new blue P&O Containers with the logo and flags in the centre was set up at this temporary site. Geoff Lock, Terminal Manager for P&O Containers had the task of getting them all shunted from the Container Terminal and placed alongside the railway line where the Queen would arrive. Everything was in place when an overnight storm blew a couple of containers over the track. Geoff had to hastily arrange for the removal of the damaged containers and organise replacements. Luckily there were some on site, but it caused a few stressful moments! The marquees can be seen being disassembled here. (*Andrew Sassoli-Walker*)

Officers line the promenade deck of *Oriana* to watch HM the Queen officially name the ship, 6 April 1995. (*Alan Mackenzie*)

The Royal Standard flying from *Oriana*'s mast on Naming Day, 1995. (*Alan Mackenzie*)

Top: HM the Queen, accompanied by HRH the Duke of Edinburgh and Lord and Lady Sterling, arrives to name *Oriana*, 6 April 1995. (*Alan Mackenzie*)

Bottom: The ceremonial sword, presented to Commodore Gibb in the presence of HM the Queen, by Lord Sterling, following the naming of *Oriana*, 1995. (*Andrew Sassoli-Walker*)

Opposite: A firework display rounds off the Naming Day for *Oriana*. (*Andrew Sassoli-Walker*)

Above: *Oriana* lies at her naming berth dressed overall, prior to moving back to the Mayflower Cruise Terminal and embarking passengers for her maiden voyage, April 1995. (*Andrew Sassoli-Walker*)

Opposite: Oriana is surrounded by small craft sending her off on her maiden voyage in style. (*Andrew Sassoli-Walker*)

Right: Oriana picks up speed down Southampton Water on her way to Funchal, Madeira, the first port of call on the maiden voyage. (*Andrew Sassoli-Walker*)

During the maiden voyage, Lord Sterling and Commodore Gibb met each morning for coffee around 1100hrs in a cordoned off area of The Conservatory, to go through the Chairman's latest list of issues to be resolved! He frequently sailed on the ships to see what was happening and to talk to passengers. One event Commodore Gibb recalled occurred at La Manga – the golf resort near Cartagena in Spain which was then owned by P&O. Sir Jeffrey went off there for the day accompanied by the Staff Capt., Hamish Reid and the Chief Engineer, Marcus James. As the ship's departure time drew near, Sir Jeffrey drew up beside *Oriana* in a taxi, but there was no sign of the two officers. It transpired that he had taken the only taxi around, while the other two had to make their own way back to the ship, which could not put to sea without them! Commodore Gibb made an announcement explaining the reason for the delay in sailing and asked the passengers to line the rails and all cheer when they finally returned!

Mark Thomas was a passenger on the maiden voyage with his wife Nicola. He recalls, 'The build-up to the launch of *Oriana* was significant, as befitted the first cruise ship designed for the UK market. More so perhaps when one considers that in the early 1990s corporate websites and on-demand access to news did not exist. Her entry into service received wide newspaper, radio and television coverage – even an *Oriana* supplement in the *Times* newspaper.'

Page from the maiden season brochure for *Oriana*, with one of the early computer-aided design images of the ship, 1995. (*Sharon Poole collection*)

Enjoy a cocktail in Oriana's Crow's Nest Bar.

INTRODUCING THE GREATEST BRITISH LINER

Oriana has been eight years in the planning. But, when you step aboard into her soaring four-deck atrium, you'll soon realise that in fact, she epitomises everything that we have learned from 150 years of cruising.

She's the largest liner ever built specifically to cruise from Britain. And she offers every comfort, every facility and every amenity that discerning cruise passengers expect - plus a range of features that exceed even the most experienced cruiser's expectations.

Her unique hull-form and high speed (she is the fastest liner built for a quarter of a century) allow her to sail swiftly and smoothly to the sun. Her wide range of public rooms, each with a different mood and atmosphere, are designed to be intimate and to offer a variety of environments, a myriad of activities.

Her sun decks are the most expansive at sea, the largest of her three pools the biggest afloat.

You'll find everything you need for the ultimate cruise, from superb shops to an elaborate health centre, from a relaxing library to a theatre incorporating the stage wizardry to make our musicals and shows more spectacular than ever, from two superb restaurants to the informal all-day dining offered in the Conservatory

But there's more to Oriana than sheer technology. We've taken enormous care to build on the success of Canberra and Sea Princess. So Oriana bears a strong family resemblance to Canberra. She's a classically beautiful ship in an era of floating apartment blocks.

Internally, her decor glows with traditional materials, rich wood and warm fabrics. And her cabins and staterooms offer all the facilities you'd expect - plus exciting new features like colour television and refrigerators and (in top grade accommodations) private balconies.

But there's more to any ship than facilities: in the end, it's the ship's company that brings any vessel to life. And Oriana benefits from a hand-picked crew, experienced in providing the exemplary service and flawless seamanship that have always characterised P&O ships.

Oriana is destined to become a firm favourite with cruise passengers old and new. Why not sail with her in her maiden season and share in the birth of a legend?

HEALTH & BEAUTY

Oriana's health and beauty spa, The Oasis, will be managed by Champneys, a name synonymous with renowned health resorts. Their expertise and knowledge will be invaluable in creating a world of top-to-toe beauty treatments.

Page 4

Oriana - 67,000 tons

Soak up the sun around the Crystal Pool.

No shipboard venue will upstage Oriana's Theatre Royal

Page 5

ORIANA

Commodore Ian Gibb and his Officers

request the pleasure of your company

at the Champagne Reception

on Monday, 10th April 1995 in the Crow's Nest

1st sitting passengers at 6.00pm
2nd sitting passengers at 8.00pm

ORIANA
Maiden Voyage

Katy Morgan, the P.O.S.H. Club Secretary
requests the pleasure of your company

for a Champagne Reception
Friday, 21st April 199...
First sitting passengers at 19...
Second sitting pass...
in the...

ORIANA

1st edition **Sunday, 9th April 1995**

TODAY

GENERAL EMERGENCY STATIONS DRILL

At 5.00pm today . . .

. . . . an emergency drill will be held. It is a requirement of law that after boarding the ship, **all passengers** must attend and be instructed at their General Emergency Stations.

On commencement of this exercise, broadcasts will be made, and alarm bells will be sounded, calling you to your muster stations, as indicated on the notice behind your cabin door. Please carry your life-jacket with you, do not wear it and for safety's sake do not allow the ties to trail on the deck. The correct method of wearing a life-jacket will be demonstrated to you at the end of this muster.

During this exercise Champneys, the Shops, Bars, Peter Pan's and the Reception Desk will be closed. We apologise for any resulting delay in resuming the ship's services and thank you for your cooperation in these matters of safety.

DRESS FOR TODAY

Casual. Open necked shirts and long trousers for gentlemen; slacks or casual day dress for ladies.

Welcome Aboard Oriana

Commodore Ian Gibb

and the Ship's Company welcome you on board for this very special cruise. I hope that the holiday will be a memorable and exciting one - we will do all we can to make it so. It will be an experience and an adventure for all of us . . . welcome once again.

Senior Officers

Staff Captain	Phil Pickford
Chief Engineer Officer	Marcus James
Purser	Chris Bullen
Doctor	Stuart Fleming
Cruise Director	Ian Fraser
Safety Officer	Bill Kent
First Engineer	Paul Carney
Second Engineer Officer	Jeff Talbot
Chief Electro Technical Officer	John Gunner
Deputy Purser Food & Beverage	James Cusick
Deputy Purser Administration	Louise Dowds
Deputy Purser Accommodation	Rod Blackman
Chef de Cuisine	David McLachlan
First Officer	Julian Burgess
Deputy Cruise Director	Ross Howard

Far left: Photograph of *Oriana* at the entrance to Southampton Water with some invitations issued to those on the maiden voyage. (*Mark Thomas collection*)

Left: The very first edition of *Oriana Today*, 9 April 1995. (*Mark Thomas collection*)

Mark continues, 'We had looked forward to the maiden voyage for years. Despite gleaning all we could about her from advance publicity, nothing could have prepared us for our first impressions on boarding. Gone was that world of P&O ocean liners we knew so well. Here was a fresh new ship with the latest facilities but which somehow managed to retain all that tradition in her décor and an ocean liner pedigree in her design. A ship designed for fast deep-ocean cruising and long ocean passages while maintaining the acres of outside deck space so appreciated by British passengers in almost all weathers. We take so much for granted in terms of facilities on new cruise ships and they continue to evolve with every newbuild. Back in 1995 *Oriana* was not evolutionary; she was such a step-change in all respects she was in her time revolutionary. *Oriana* paved the way for the cruising product we enjoy today and in that respect deserves recognition as another P&O Cruises ship that shaped the future.'

Mark and Nicola paid £4,500 for an inside cabin on the maiden voyage, which they considered good value, particularly in view of the additional on-board facilities compared with *Canberra*. This is a mark of how prices have fallen over the intervening years in real terms. There were a few technical issues while everyone – crew and passengers – got used to the new ship. One cause of some frustration was that the toasters for the Conservatory had been left on the quayside in Southampton! Other minor issues were caused by the ship's late arrival in Southampton and consequent hasty loading of stores. For example, they knew they had soup ladles on board – they just couldn't find them! There were occasional power outages, and on one occasion Commodore Gibb made his normal pre-departure talk over the public address system, announcing the delay in sailing due to the engineer having lost electricity, but reassured everyone that he should find it shortly! As Executive Purser Chris Bullen messaged *Canberra*, 'A few teething problems but the dentist has been busy?'

THE COMMODORE'S
GALA DINNER

ON BOARD M.V. ORIANA
DURING HER MAIDEN VOYAGE

FRIDAY, 21ST APRIL 1995

FROM THE WINE CELLAR

BOLLINGER SPECIAL CUVÉE BRUT N.V. - £25.00
The traditional Champagne - dry, yet full-bodied, with a clean finish

WHITE: PULIGNY-MONTRACHET 1988 CHÂTEAU DE PULIGNY-MONTRACHET DOMAINE BOTTLED - £22.00
A well-balanced, tender, mellow wine with excellent flavours and finesse

RED: GEVREY-CHAMBERTIN DOMAINE JEAN TAUPENOT 1990 - £20.00
Aristocratic well-bred wine, ready for drinking now

Avocado Pear with Oranges, Sour Cream and Cinnamon
Smoked Scottish Salmon with Capers and Lemon

Lightly Spiced Parsnip and Apple Soup
Consommé with Chicken, Noodles and Peas

Half a Grilled Lobster with Hazelnut, Lemon and Herb Butter

Champagne Sorbet

Roast Fillet of Beef Wellington with Perigordine Sauce

Milk Fed Calf's Liver served with a reduction of Cream Shallots and Raspberry Vinegar

Spinach and Stilton Pancakes with Onion Sauce

M Baked Breast of Chicken with Sesame Crust and Braised Cabbage Leaves

Cauliflower   Panache of Vegetables

Steamed Potatoes   Roast Potatoes

Fresh Strawberries Romanoff
Choux Pastry Swans on a Praline Sauce
Compote of Guavas
M Rich Chocolate and Cherry Cheesecake

Selection of British and Continental Cheeses with Onion Bread and Fresh Fruit

Freshly Brewed Coffee   De-Caffeinated   Speciality Teas
Petit Fours

A selection of Rolls

M DENOTES A SPECIALITY DISH FROM OUR CONSULTANT CHEF, ANTON MOSIMANN

TROPICAL CARNIVAL DINNER

M.V. ORIANA
MAIDEN CRUISE

SUNDAY, 16TH APRIL 1995

Spiced Prawn and Lychee Cocktail

Roasted Banana with Hot and Sour Compote

Avocado Pear Cantabrios with a Light Fruit and Yoghurt Dressing

Caribbean Chicken and Corn Soup

Chilled Pepperpot Soup with Sour Cream

Blackened Seared Halibut in Cajun Spices with Lime Butter

Rib Eye Steak Mardi Gras with a Creole Sauce

Smoked Loin of Pork Carib

Gumbo - suggested as a vegetarian dish

Glazed Carved Joints with Summer Salads and Dips

Baked Potatoes

Hot 'n' Spicy Roasters

Cauliflower and Baby Corn

Roast Vegetables

Jamaican Style Baked Pineapple

Tropical Baba with Orange Curacao Sauce

Coconut Chocolate Suprise

Compote of Tropical Fruits in Ginger Syrup

Papaya Sorbet

Selection of British and Continental Cheeses
with Black Bun and Fresh Fruit

Freshly Brewed Coffee   De-caffeinated
Speciality Teas
Island Sweetmeats

From the Bakery - a selection of Rolls

Wines

Champagne: Bollinger Special Cuvee Brut n v - £25.00

White: Frascati Superiore Fontana Candida 1992, 1993 - £7.00

Red: Barolo Fontanafredda 1989, 1990 - £11.50

Left: The menu for the Commodore's Gala Dinner on the maiden voyage of *Oriana*, 21 April 1995. (*Michael Whittingham collection*)

Above: Menu for the Tropical Carnival Dinner on the maiden voyage of *Oriana*, 16 April 1995. (*Peter Smith collection*)

Far left: One of the 86,000 pieces of Wedgwood china specially made for *Oriana*. (*Sharon Poole collection*)

Left: Cover and inset of *The Cruise*. (*Andrew Sassoli-Walker collection*)

With *Oriana* came lots of small changes that were probably unnoticed by the general public. For example, engineers wore khaki uniforms in public areas, rather than their traditional white boiler suits, which were now reserved for machinery areas. The branding for P&O Cruises also now had the rising sun emblem rather than the P&O house flag, a logo which in its new form still symbolises the brand.

If there is one piece of music that has come to represent *Oriana* it is 'Conquest of Paradise' by Vangelis. Commodore Gibb first heard it being played on the handover of the vessel in Emden. From that moment, this melody was played on departure from every port on the maiden voyage, and even in various television programmes that featured *Oriana*.

In 1993 Sue Kilbracken, fund-raiser for the Dyslexia Institute (DI), had the idea of asking a variety of authors to write a novel which could be sold to raise money for the DI. After consulting various people it was decided that it should be a contemporary novel with the linking factor being that is should be set either in a school or on board a cruise ship. Various companies were approached for help and it was P&O Cruises who warmed most to the idea, especially since publication would coincide with the launch of *Oriana*. Fourteen authors signed up to each write one chapter, including such household names as Maeve Binchy, Bernard Cornwell, Ken Follett and Joanna Trollope. For their part, P&O Cruises stipulated just one condition – that in the story, the ship should not be sunk or hijacked. The result was *The Cruise*, a novel of murder and romance, set on a voyage to the Mediterranean on board *Oriana*. It has a remarkable continuity considering the wide variety of writing styles of the authors, the fact that the ship had not then been completed and not one of the authors had ever embarked on a cruise! I wonder how many readers decided to sail on *Oriana* as a result of reading this book.

Chapter 5

IT'S NOT LIKE *CANBERRA*!

When passengers find a comfortable and happy ship, they can become so attached to it that the idea of change is sometimes difficult. The late Sir Hugh Casson recognised this in an article he wrote for the *Architectural Review* in 1969 when he said, 'Ships alone invite and receive an affection that is almost personal in its intensity.' Despite the obvious inconveniences such as communal bathrooms and somewhat crowded facilities, many had become devoted to *Canberra,* which had achieved an almost legendary status following her triumphant return from service as a troop carrier and hospital ship in the Falklands Conflict in 1982. However, despite spending her later years as a one-class cruise ship, nothing could change the fact that *Canberra* was built in 1961 as a two-class liner mainly for the emigrant run to Australia. *Oriana* was first and foremost a single-class, or rather classless, cruise ship.

Carl Ilardi recalled a transatlantic voyage he and his wife took on *Oriana* in 2000. 'We sailed from Southampton to New York and had a great time! We were among only a small group of Americans aboard the ship, certainly less than ten. I will always remember being in a queue when I overheard a couple of dowagers complaining about a spot of turbulent sea that we had encountered. "We NEVER had weather like this on *Canberra!*" they groused, as if the newer ship was totally responsible for their discomfort.' This became almost a mantra among some passengers in the early years. Tom O'Connor had the whole theatre on *Oriana* erupting with laughter when as part of his performance on the maiden voyage, he asked the audience how many times they had heard, "It's not like this on *Canberra!*"'

Indeed, *Oriana* was NOT like *Canberra,* although in the liner tradition, out of the 914 cabins, 112 were designated for single occupancy. These rooms were the same size as twin cabins and as such were converted for twin occupancy around 2001 (in the 2011 refit, two single inside cabins were built in an area once occupied by the children's clubs). There were also eight cabins specially adapted for people with disabilities. Every cabin had a colour television, safe, direct-dial telephone, refrigerator and

en-suite bath or shower room. There were eight suites and sixteen mini-suites. Of the remaining twin cabins, 118 had balconies. Since *Oriana* was specifically designed for cruises of up to three months duration, storage in the cabins was generous, each with a minimum of twelve drawers in addition to hanging space

Frequent cruisers would certainly have noticed the new restaurant menus and there was some concern as to how passengers would react to them at first. In the event they responded well to the greater variety and lighter food created by Swiss chef Anton Mosimann, although P&O Cruises' staples such as roasts and proper puddings remained available, as did the very popular lunchtime curries. Mark Thomas recalls his

A table overlooking the stern in *Oriana's* Oriental Restaurant.
(*Andrew Sassoli-Walker*)

delight in sitting in the Oriental Restaurant and having a sea view. On *Canberra*, there were no windows in the Atlantic Restaurant. Another major innovation on *Oriana* was an alternative to the main restaurant in the form of the option to dine informally at night in The Conservatory. Many of these evenings were themed according to the ports of call.

The health and beauty spa, located in an attractive bright position at the top of the ship, was managed by Champneys. Again, it was something fresh to have a fully-equipped spa on board offering a wide range of treatments, after *Canberra's* limited massage, beauty and hair-dressing salon.

Of her public rooms, perhaps the most beautiful was the Curzon Room. Specially designed for classical music recitals, its centrepiece was a Steinway grand piano, while the room was illuminated by striking crystal chandeliers. It was not easy to ensure good acoustics in this comparatively low-ceilinged space spanning the full width of the ship, but careful design coupled with a state-of-the-art amplification system resulted in a performance which could be heard perfectly from any seat. Over the years, this room has seen some changes and after being a signature restaurant for Gary Rhodes for some years, is now Marco Pierre White's Ocean Grill. The unique décor of the room remains unchanged however.

Another of *Oriana's* most striking features was the quantity and quality of original art on board – nearly 3,000 pieces – decorating the public rooms and walkways as well as individual crew and passenger cabins. All the artworks

Above: The Curzon Room on *Oriana,* shown in its original form as a venue for classical piano recitals. (*Stuart McGregor*)

Right: Sparkling tableware at *Oriana* Rhodes at the Curzon Room. The venue was converted from a venue for classical music recitals into a fine dining restaurant in 2006. (*Andrew Sassoli-Walker*)

were by contemporary British or Commonwealth artists working in a variety of mediums – ceramics, sculpture, textiles and painting – the majority of which were specially commissioned for the ship. The largest painting was the 17-metre long, oil-on-canvas triptych, the *Journey of Odysseus* by Rose Waroch, mounted in the Peninsular Restaurant. To augment the modern art, there were also a number of period British watercolour landscapes and cartoons in some of the public areas such as the Library and Curzon Room. In the ship's early years of service a self-guided tour leaflet was given to passengers so that they could learn more about the inspiration and provenance of each piece. A souvenir book was also published, giving readers further insight into the art.

As on *Canberra,* younger passengers were not forgotten, but there any similarity ended. *Oriana* catered for up to 200 children in the summer

Above: Rose Waroch's epic painting entitled *The Journey of Odysseus,* on the wall of *Oriana's* Peninsular restaurant. This 17-metre oil-on-canvas painting is the largest piece of art on board. (*Andrew Sassoli-Walker*)

RIght: The Crystal Pool, *Oriana.* The bronze and copper sculpture, entitled *Boating*, is by André Wallace. At the time of her launch, this was the largest swimming pool afloat. (*Andrew Sassoli-Walker*)

These pages, from top left: The entrance to Chaplin's Cinema, *Oriana*. The two resin figures of Charlie Chaplin are by John Clinch. (*Andrew Sassoli-Walker*)

Chaplin's cinema, *Oriana*. As well as screening films, this is also the venue for port presentations and other talks. (*Andrew Sassoli-Walker*)

Gleaming in the sunshine, *Oriana* is a welcome sight to passengers returning from a day ashore at Lanzarote, November 2007. (*Andrew Sassoli-Walker*)

The sweeping curves of the stern decks of *Oriana* with the Terrace Pool in the foreground. (*David Raymonde*)

These pages, from left: Sweeping curves and teak decking epitomise *Oriana*. (*Andrew Sassoli-Walker*)

Looking up towards the Tiffany-style glass ceiling in the atrium of *Oriana*. (*Andrew Sassoli-Walker*)

The entrance to Anderson's Bar on *Oriana*. This elegant venue has the atmosphere of a gentlemen's club with comfortable sofas and winged armchairs. (*Stuart McGregor*)

Lord's Tavern on *Oriana*, created in homage to *Canberra*'s Cricketer's Bar. In the mid-twentieth century P&O used to carry the England cricket team to Australia. (*Andrew Sassoli-Walker*)

This page: The highly-polished sprung dance floor in Harlequins on *Oriana* caters for ballroom dancers in the evening, becoming a night club into the small hours. (*Sharon Poole*)

The engraved glass doors of Peter Pan's, *Oriana*, illustrating characters from the popular children's book by J. M. Barrie. This area, once catering for children up to the age of nine, was converted into cabins when *Oriana* became an adult-only ship in 2011. (*Andrew Sassoli-Walker*)

Peter Pan's, one of three children's facilities on *Oriana*, each catering for a different age range. This was for the two to nine year olds. (*Andrew Sassoli-Walker*)

holidays and there were plenty of activities for them to do. Their facilities were arranged in three distinct areas, according to different age groups – Peter Pan's for two to nine year-olds, Decibels for ten to twelve year-olds and Outer Space for thirteen to seventeen year-olds. They also had their own area of outside deck complete with paddling pool. There was a video arcade, night nursery and in-cabin baby-listening system – the latter a first for P&O Cruises at the time.

Chapter 6

PROJECT CAPRICORN – A NEW DAWN

For five years, *Oriana* sailed the oceans as the flagship of P&O Cruises, arguably as the flagship for the British merchant fleet, since by that time Cunard's legendary *Queen Elizabeth 2* was close on thirty years old. The rest of the P&O Cruises fleet then consisted of *Canberra* and *Sea Princess,* later renamed *Victoria*. In 1997, *Canberra* was finally retired and temporarily replaced by *Star Princess*, which was transferred over from Princess Cruises and renamed *Arcadia* (the third P&O vessel to be so named). All the while plans were being made for a new ship and a sister to *Oriana*. This was codenamed Project Capricorn, occasionally referred to as *Oriana 2*.

However the ship, to be called *Aurora,* would not be an identical twin sister. While *Oriana* would be the reference ship, rapid changes in the cruise market led to a number of improvements so that instead of building another *Oriana, Aurora* became an entirely new design. The major difference was with the propulsion and engine arrangement. Instead of utilising diesel-mechanical engines as on *Oriana*, it was decided to use the, by then more common, diesel-electric engines. Four MAN B&W diesel engines each drive their own alternator and can produce up to fourteen megawatts of electrical power, which is transferred to two main drive electric motors to power the shafts. Another technical difference between the two ships is that instead of variable-pitch propellers, *Aurora* has fixed-pitch blades. Her twin rudders may be operated simultaneously or independently and she has a fully-enclosed bridge. Charles Arkinstall: '*Aurora* was very much an updated version of *Oriana* with a change in the propulsion system to diesel-electric (something we wanted to do with *Oriana* but nether P&O Cruises nor Meyer Werft had experience of diesel-electric at the time), along with many more balcony cabins, a much improved arrangement of the sports deck, larger atrium, an alternate dining venue and a few other adjustments to public spaces based on in-service experience with *Oriana*, but the ships have many similarities too.'

Opposite: Watercolour entitled *I saw Three Ships* by Andrew Dibben. This shows the P&O Cruises fleet as it was in 1995 – *Oriana*, *Canberra* and *Victoria*. It was used as a POSH Club Christmas card in *Oriana's* maiden year. (*Andrew Sassoli-Walker collection*)

Above: *Aurora* sets sail for the USA and Canada on a glorious September afternoon, 2009. (*Andrew Sassoli-Walker*)

Right: Senior officers watch the early evening views of Venice from *Aurora's* port bridge wing, 2007. (*Steve Matthews*)

Above: Aurora, at anchor at Spitsbergen, June 2009. (*Bob Walker*)

Opposite left: Aurora's engine room, showing one of the four MAN B&W diesel-electric engines. (The Ship's Photographer)

Opposite right: View of *Aurora's* twin propellers and rudders. Unlike *Oriana, Aurora* was fitted with fixed-pitch propellers and independently controllable rudders. (*David Jewkes*)

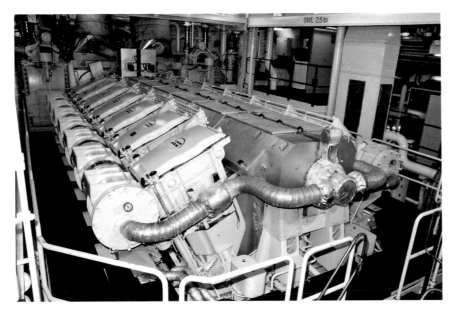

A sliding glass roof or magradome encloses *Aurora*'s Crystal Pool, allowing its use in almost all weathers. A shallow paddling pool was also added to *Aurora*, next to the Terrace Pool on D Deck. Regarding passenger accommodation, *Aurora* has 939 cabins against *Oriana*'s 914, some of which are interconnecting for family use. Additionally, 60 per cent of *Aurora*'s outside cabins have private balconies so, while *Oriana* has just one deck of this grade of cabin, *Aurora* has three decks, plus another twenty-four cabins forward on Lido Deck. These extra balconies were cleverly incorporated into the design by widening the beam of the ship above the Promenade Deck, so still giving the versatility of being able to transit the Panama Canal when required. However, Charles

Arkinstall recalls, 'The Panama Canal authorities were, for a period, giving approval to ships which exceeded the thirty-two metres limitation provided the extension did not in any way impede the operation of the mules running up and down the locks to which the ships are moored. I cannot remember which ship/cruise line first 'broke' the rules but we were, at the time, building the Sun Princess class at Fincantieri and had sought and obtained the agreement of the Canal to widen the ship in this way. We built four of this class and had to seek approval each time. I do remember we had a struggle to get approval for the last in the series (and thereafter they insisted that there were no more protrusions) but *Aurora* fell somewhere in the middle of these and we got the necessary

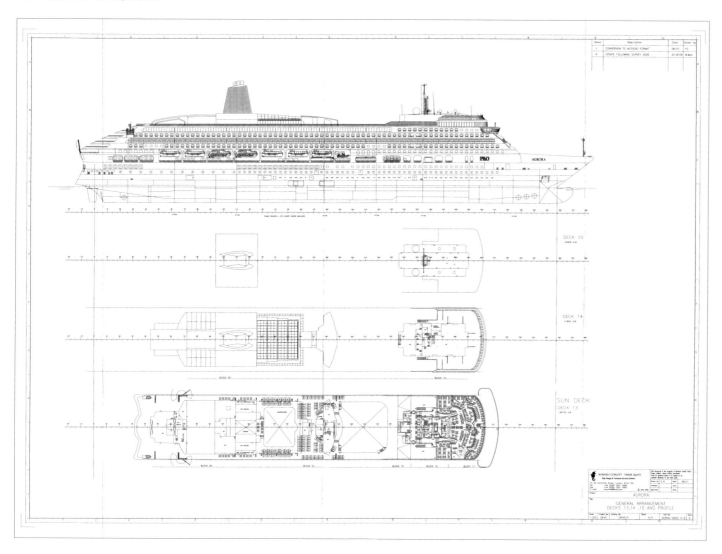

DECK 15

DECK 14

SUN DECK
DECK 13

Opposite: Part of *Aurora's* General Arrangement plan showing the design differences from *Oriana.* (Carnival UK)

Above: The retractable magradome over *Aurora's* Crystal Pool. (*Andrew Sassoli-Walker*)

Right: A curved staircase leads down from the bedroom to the lounge in one of the two Penthouse Suites on *Aurora.* This is the Library Suite with choice of books and audio discs. (*Andrew Sassoli-Walker*)

Above: The lounge and dining area of one of the two Penthouse Suites on *Aurora*, complete with baby grand piano. The staircase leads up to the bedroom, dressing room and bathroom with whirlpool bath. (*Andrew Sassoli-Walker*)

Right: *Aurora* entering one of the locks in the Panama Canal. This clearly shows her wider beam above the level of the promenade deck and how it was designed to clear the mules to which the ships are moored during the transit. (*The Ship's Photographer*)

Opposite left: *Aurora* pictured from fleet sister *Victoria* as they enter the Gatun Locks of the Panama Canal, 20 January 2001. The two vertical windows under the bridge belong to the duplex Penthouse suites. (*Alan Mackenzie*)

by Francis Design, one of the foremost luxury yacht design studios in the world.

Charles Arkinstall again headed up P&O Cruises' Technical Services Support Group. 'The order for *Aurora* was very much welcomed by all of us involved in the build process and my recollections are that the contract proceeded without any significant problems until the maiden voyage when we had to abort the cruise, but even then Meyer Werft's team responded in a way that perhaps only a German workforce is capable of doing. Papenburg remained a difficult place to access by commercial air services but we were fortunate in often having the use of the P&O aircraft to move between Southampton and the nearest airport at Gronigen, thereby saving many thousands of man hours over the course of the project. It was also particularly helpful when flying architects on hourly rates to and from the yard. It was a pleasure to work with Meyer Werft given their facility in Papenburg and the quality they produced and I was forever disappointed that we were never able to place a Princess order there.'

On Tuesday, 15 December 1998, on a wet and miserable day, the first 400 ton block of the keel of *Aurora*, or Hull No. 640 as she was then, was laid down in the covered building dock in the Papenburg shipyard of Meyer Werft. The then Managing Director of P&O Cruises, Gwyn Hughes, laid down a one pound coin and Bernard Meyer of Meyer Werft, a German one mark coin on the keel blocks before the hull section was placed into position by the yard´s 600 ton crane, in the time-honoured ceremony.

Watching the proceedings were P&O Cruises Marketing Director David Dingle, and other directors of Meyer Werft together with invited guests and representatives of international tour operators and journalists. In the same method used for *Oriana,* prefabricated sections of hull were prepared in an assembly shop, hoisted into position by crane and welded together.

agreement. The Panamanians would not give approval at the time of contract but only in advance of the first transit so there was always a certain anxiety that one had built a ship for regular canal transit but which still required this dispensation to be granted.' In another first for P&O Cruises, *Aurora* also has two duplex penthouse suites with forward views from floor-to-ceiling windows and balconies on both levels.

As with *Oriana*, the four design teams were co-ordinated by Robert Tillberg and Meyer Werft again won the contract to build her. Jim Hunter comments, 'For *Oriana* there were limitations in that *Canberra* still loomed large in the P&O psyche. Greater latitude was allowed for *Aurora* and a professional 'profiler' was engaged, and accounts for some of the differences between the two ships.' *Aurora*'s final profile lines were drawn

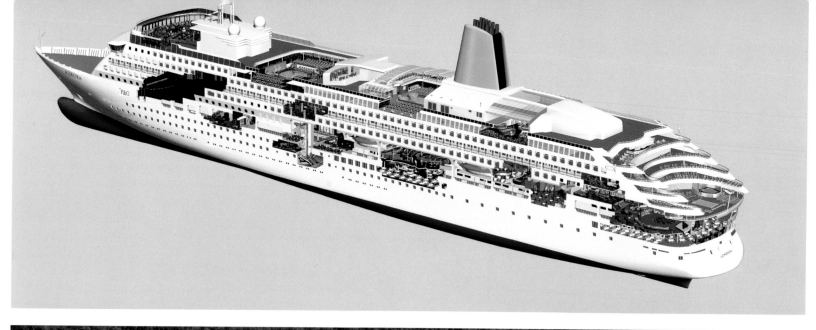

Newbuilding S.640

MEYER WERFT

Jos. L. Meyer GmbH
Shipbuilders and Engineers
Papenburg Germany
2000

Opposite top: Cut-away diagram of *Aurora.* (P&O Cruises)

Opposite bottom: The elegant profile of *Aurora* is seen clearly as she tenders passengers ashore in the calm of the Norwegian fjords, 2009. (*Bob Walker*)

Above: The builder's plate on *Aurora.* (*Andrew Sassoli-Walker*)

Her first master was Capt. Steve Burgoine. Having worked for P&O Cruises for over thirty years, he was promoted to captain in 1996 and at the time of his posting to *Aurora,* was in command of *Oriana.* As with Commodore Gibb and *Oriana*, Capt. Burgoine joined the ship while she was in the final build stage and was living on board from February 2000 so that he could familiarise himself with the ship and her systems and prepare for her maiden season.

In December 1999, the dock was flooded and *Aurora* took to the water for the first time. At this stage the ship was fitted with two dummy propellers with zero-thrust so that the engines and machinery could be tested in the flooded dock without moving the vessel. Then the two twenty-ton Swedish propellers were lifted into position. Each of the five blades measured 4.5 square metres.

In the early hours of 18 January 2000, Hull No. 640 was inched out of the huge building dock which had been her home for the previous thirteen months. As she reversed out, the 64-ton aluminium funnel was hoisted high into the air and the vessel edged backwards until she was in the correct position for it to be lowered onto the top deck, making *Aurora* 53 metres from waterline to the top of the funnel. This houses the vents that discharge the hot gases from the power plants and the galley ovens, as well as containing a heat-recovery system which generates steam used to heat bath water and air conditioning units. Hull No. 640 could now be seen in all her glory.

Aurora was then towed to the fitting-out berth for completion. Whereas the interior styling of *Oriana* had been traditional with much use made of polished wood and brass, *Aurora* was more contemporary in décor to appeal to a younger cruise market. The same design team worked on *Aurora* as on *Oriana* – Petter Yran for the cabins and John McNeece for the public rooms.

In August 1999 the Executive Purser, Brian Purnell, and his team began to calculate the amount of equipment and supplies that would be required to feed the 2,724 mouths on every cruise (passengers and crew). Any brand new ship has to be stocked from scratch so this is done in phases right up to the final preparations for the maiden voyage. At each stage she is supplied with just enough food and drink for the building teams and crew that are actually on board. The first phase was to cover the river transit out for her sea trials, which took place on 19 February

Opposite left: Engine tests on *Aurora* using zero-thrust temporary propellers, while she was still in the building dock. (Meyer Werft)

Opposite right: One of the two huge bronze propellers fitted to *Aurora*. The propellers are fixed-pitch, with the rudders (left) independently controllable. (The Ship's Photographer)

Above: One of the two stabiliser fins on *Aurora*. Each fin is a little over six metres in length. A computer senses the roll of the ship and automatically adjusts the angle of the fins to counteract the wave motion. (The Ship's Photographer)

Right: Cranes lift the funnel into place on *Aurora* as she is edged backwards out of the building dock. (Meyer Werft)

These pages: Shipyard workers pose for a photo after the funnel is welded into position on *Aurora. (*Meyer Werft*)*

Aerial view of *Aurora* in the fitting-out berth at the Meyer Werft shipyard at Papenburg. (Meyer Werft)

Aurora under construction in the Meyer Werft fitting-out berth. (*Robert Lloyd*)

The foredeck of *Aurora,* still under construction but with the crew swimming pool nearly complete. (*Robert Lloyd*)

Above left: View over the Riviera Pool and Sun Deck of *Aurora,* while in the Meyer Werft fitting-out berth. (*Robert Lloyd*)

Above right: View over *Aurora's* Riviera Pool with the mast under construction. (Robert Lloyd)

2000. At this point only essential supplies and hotel equipment were loaded, such as some crockery, glassware, fresh meat, dairy produce, fruit and vegetables and soft drinks. No alcohol was allowed on board as she was still technically under construction and in the ownership of Meyer Werft.

As previously mentioned, the shipyard is situated on the tidal part of the River Ems, which was once again specially dredged for the occasion. Even so, it was vital to keep the ship's weight to a minimum due to the shallows that *Aurora* would have to negotiate. Indeed, when she reached the halfway point of Leer on an ebbing tide, she would have to moor

and wait for the tide to rise again to continue her journey to the sea. She was also carrying no ballast and had the least amount of fuel and stores possible, but despite these preparations there was just one metre of water under the keel at one point. The river transit was an event in its own right as this huge ship appeared to sail through the flooded fields. The railway bridge had to be dismantled yet again to allow her to pass, and there was just four metres clearance either side between the bridge supports. The whole journey was undertaken under her own power with Meyer Werft captain Friedheim Husemeyer in command, assisted by a local river pilot. There were also two tugs in attendance in case of need. For those who

The carpet being fitted at the foot of the main stairs in *Aurora's* atrium. (Meyer Werft)

could not make the journey to watch this event, Meyer Werft set up two webcams and broadcast the journey over the internet. It was estimated that over 10,000 people watched in this way. Finally, just before dawn, Hull No. 640 was safely moored at Emshaven, where the funnel uptakes were added, thus giving *Aurora* her final appearance.

The first set of sea trials are the Builder's Trials and enabled the yard team to fine-tune the equipment and on-board systems as well as perform all the regulatory tests required such as anchor testing, compass adjustments and calibration of navigational equipment. During this period P&O Cruises' officers are purely observers and the ship is handled by Meyer Werft crew. The second series of sea trials are the Owner's Acceptance Trials which include extreme manoeuvres such as crash stops from her full speed of 25 knots, turning circles and the most stomach-churning of all – using the stabilisers in reverse to induce roll to assess their effectiveness. All this would be assessed to determine noise levels, vibration and general manoeuvrability.

During both trials, interior fitting-out continued and the hotel services crew began to familiarise themselves with equipment and routines. *Aurora* passed all her tests with flying colours. Capt. Steve Burgoine commented, 'I am immensely looking forward to bringing *Aurora* out and I feel privileged to be given the opportunity. She is going to be a fine ship and so far the sea trials have proved her to be a very stable and comfortable ship ... The bridge layout and technology is awesome and it will be rewarding to set up new routines to operate the ship.'

Now *Aurora* could be fully equipped. This included carpet laying and completing the furnishings. Some 14,450 napkins, 27,800 towels, 47,800 coat hangers and cabin toiletries were all brought on board from where they had been stored in warehouses in Emshaven in Holland. The final topping-up of stores would take place in Southampton just prior to the maiden voyage.

Above: Aurora transiting the River Ems from the Meyer Werft shipyard to begin sea trials, 2000. (*Alan Mackenzie*)

Right: John Mills' Lalique-style waterfall, in the magnificent atrium on *Aurora. (Andrew Sassoli-Walker)*

Opposite *above left:* The hand-over ceremony for *Aurora,* with the crew lined up on the aft decks as the Red Ensign is raised for the first time. (Meyer Werft)

Opposite above right: Aurora speeds through the English Channel, en route to her new home of Southampton, 22 April 2000. (*Alan Mackenzie*)

Opposite below right: Aurora, seen from lifeboat No.9 during crew drill off Teignmouth, Devon, 23 April 2000. (*Alan Mackenzie*)

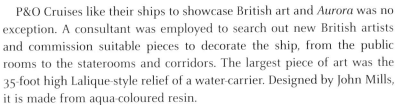

P&O Cruises like their ships to showcase British art and *Aurora* was no exception. A consultant was employed to search out new British artists and commission suitable pieces to decorate the ship, from the public rooms to the staterooms and corridors. The largest piece of art was the 35-foot high Lalique-style relief of a water-carrier. Designed by John Mills, it is made from aqua-coloured resin.

On 14 April 2000, *Aurora* was officially handed over from Meyer Werft to P&O Cruises and set sail for her new home port of Southampton, arriving two days later to berth at the Queen Elizabeth II Terminal. *Aurora* was the first new cruise ship of the Millennium and brought the P&O Cruises fleet up to four vessels, each with a distinctive and unique character.

Above left: *Aurora's* crew become acquainted with their new home on the shakedown cruise from Germany to Southampton, 22 April 2000. (*Alan Mackenzie*)

Above right: RFD Marin-Ark passenger evacuation system, pictured in a demonstration on *Celebrity Eclipse*. While many ferries had already been installed with this system, *Aurora* marked a turning point for the industry as it was the first cruise vessel to be so equipped. One special feature of this equipment is that it can be installed and launched from internal passenger decks, unlike lifeboats which must be installed on open weather decks. Evacuees can muster and evacuate from the safety of passenger areas without risk or exposure to the elements. (RFD Beaufort, Survitec Group)

Left: Aurora's tender platforms in use. Following success with using this type of tender platform (which opens outwards using hydraulic rams) on Princess ships, they were installed on both *Oriana* and *Aurora*. Richard Vie commented that, 'It is quite a difficult feature to design as it is on the waterline so clearly the watertight integrity of the ship is an issue and minimising the space taken up by internal access routes, including arranging for wheelchair access, is challenging. Powerful hydraulics are needed to deploy what is a heavy platform (it has to withstand tender impact when deployed and sea, quay and tug forces when stowed).' Another advantage is that passengers descend to the platform using internal staircases or a lift rather than external companionways. (*Paul Newland*)

Chapter 7

NAMING AND MAIDEN VOYAGE
OF *AURORA*

AURORA: THE ROMAN GODDESS OF THE DAWN.
'Events like this truly occur only once in a millennium ... *Aurora* combines P&O's expertise with all that is most exciting in current cruise ship design. From the tip of her sweeping bow to the cascading terraces of her stern she will add a new dimension to cruising for the British passenger ...'

So read *Aurora*'s Maiden Season brochure for 2000. Despite the upturn in cruising from the UK, P&O Cruises clearly did not anticipate the addition of three more new cruise ships to their fleet at this time, with *Ventura* and *Azura* both carrying over 3,000 passengers each!

Andrew Sassoli-Walker takes up the story again. 'Sunday 16 April dawned cool and sunny as I, my parents and friends boarded the ferry to Cowes so we could watch the Tall Ships Race Parade of Sail which was scheduled to pass *Aurora*, then at anchor at Spithead, and due to make her maiden entrance into Southampton later that afternoon. It was a wonderful sight, watching the magnificent sailing ships gracefully pass

Aurora, a contrast of old and new. We then took the next ferry back to Southampton in good time to watch *Aurora* arrive.'

'As the sun started to become hazy, *Aurora* made her grand entrance, passing Calshot at 1320 hrs and entering Southampton just under an hour later, escorted by two fireboats giving the traditional water display. Hundreds of people thronged various vantage points and lined the banks to see the elegant white ship. To show her off to the maximum number of sightseers, Capt. Burgoine took her up to the Upper Swinging Ground, past Town Quay and P&O Cruises' home berth at the Mayflower Cruise Terminal – built for the original *Oriana* and *Canberra* – before turning the ship 180 degrees and sailing back to come alongside the Queen Elizabeth II Terminal where she was going to be named. Another 180 degree turn ensured her bow was facing upriver so all visitors entering Dock Gate 4, including the Princess Royal, would see her bow first.'

Opposite: On the Sunday of her maiden arrival, *Aurora* lies at anchor in the Solent for a sail past of tall ships prior to taking centre stage herself, 16 April 2000. (*Southern Daily Echo*)

Above: The Jubilee Sailing Trust's *Lord Nelson* passing *Aurora,* surrounded by a flotilla of small craft, 16 April 2000. (*Andrew Sassoli-Walker*)

Right: Aurora sails into her home port of Southampton for the first time, 16 April 2000. (*Andrew Sassoli-Walker*)

'Before *Aurora* sailed on her maiden voyage, I was able to have a look around her when Classic FM and the *Southern Daily Echo* hosted 'A Celebration of *Aurora*' concert on board. The layout was quite different from *Oriana*, and the décor more contemporary, providing an attractive background to a wonderful evening of music.'

Above: The last of the Tall Ships departs the Ocean Dock as *Aurora* moves stern first to the Queen Elizabeth II Terminal in preparation for her naming ceremony, 16 April 2000. (*Andrew Sassoli-Walker*)

Right: A celebration for Aurora was a concert held on board prior to her official naming, 19 April 2000. (*Andrew Sassoli-Walker collection*)

'I had thought that *Oriana*'s atrium was stunning, but the 10.5 metre waterfall with the Lalique-style sculpture of the Goddess of the Dawn, designed by John Mills and spanning the four-deck high atrium, was truly breath-taking, and I am forever drawn to this area when on board.'

The naming ceremony was performed by HRH the Princess Royal on 27 April 2000 in Southampton. It was preceded by a Gala Dinner on board, hosted by Lord Sterling of Plaistow, GCVO, CBE and attended by the Princess Royal, after which all guests stayed on board for a short overnight cruise, ending with a firework display. James Cusick, currently Executive

A Celebration for Aurora

Wednesday 19th April 2000

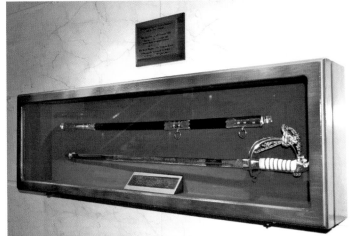

Clockwise from left:
HRH the Princess Royal
names *Aurora* amid a shower
of confetti. Unfortunately,
the champagne bottle did
not break. (*Southern Daily
Echo*)

HRH the Princess Royal
meets some P&O cadets on a
tour of *Aurora* following her
naming. (P&O Cruises)

The plaque over this
ceremonial sword, mounted
in the reception area of
Aurora reads, 'Presented to
Captain Stephen Burgoine
and his ship's company
by The Lord Sterling of
Plaistow CBE, Chairman of
The Peninsular & Oriental
Steam Navigation Company,
in the presence of Her Royal
Highness The Princess
Royal following the naming
of *Aurora*, Southampton,
27 April 2000. (*Andrew
Sassoli-Walker*)

Purser on *Aurora* and then Passenger Services Manager, remembered, 'When HRH Princess Anne came to name *Aurora* we had the great pleasure of her staying on board overnight in The Library Suite. I personally escorted the Princess along with Lord Sterling in the forward crew lifts to inspect the main laundry on Deck One. I will never forget them walking into the Accommodation Office – it was like watching a movie!' The following morning the naming ceremony took place at the Queen Elizabeth II Terminal. Unfortunately, it was slightly marred by the fact that the bottle of Champagne did not break, a fact the Press never fail to bring up whenever *Aurora* makes the news. Although problems have occurred only a handful of times against the hundreds of thousands of trouble free miles, they still like to refer to her as a 'jinxed ship' for this one reason. Just to dispel this myth, another quiet naming ceremony took place the following day. James Cusick again: 'We who sail the wonders of the deep know all about

This page: The Dawning of Aurora magazines, maiden season brochure, embarkation notice, ticket and first edition of *Aurora Today*. (*Andrew Sassoli-Walker collection*)

Champagne flutes at the ready as *Aurora* sets sail on a shorter than expected maiden voyage! (*Andrew Sassoli-Walker*)

Aurora leaving on her maiden voyage, 1815hrs, 1 May 2000. (*Michael Whittingham*)

the majesty and power of the sea. We seafarers are a God fearing and superstitious breed and it was deemed unlucky for the bottle not to break. Word quickly spread to Capt. Burgoine that the lower decks were unhappy and he hastily arranged for another unofficial naming ceremony for the ship's company. The next morning all the officers and crew gathered on the dockside as *Aurora* was named again by a cabin stewardess from Romania whose name was fortuitously Aurora! This time the bottle broke and everyone gave three cheers for the 'Goddess of the Dawn' that is *Aurora*! This was our quiet day as there were no functions booked so that Team *Aurora* could rest and prepare for the maiden voyage.'

The maiden voyage was a cruise to the Western Mediterranean leaving on 1 May 2000 and calling at Lisbon, Barcelona, Monte Carlo, Livorno, Naples, Ajaccio and Gibraltar. Among the passengers were Judith Chalmers and a TV film crew for the holiday programme *Wish You Were Here*. Andrew Sassoli-Walker takes up the story again. 'I was also on board with my parents, the Thomas family and another friend, Steve Matthews, with his parents. We embarked *Aurora* on a sunny Bank Holiday Monday, full of excitement and anticipation of the adventure ahead.

'Once our cases were unpacked and after muster drill, we all went on deck for a wonderful sailaway, knowing we were the first fare-paying passengers on board. The Essex Caledonian Band had the stirring sound of the bagpipes echoing round the berth, as a large crowd of people on the quayside waved to friends on board.

'We were all eager to get underway and finally Capt. Steve Burgoine called the crew to stations and, once singled up, all lines were dropped, and we were on our way! *Aurora*'s whistle thundered out over the city as she edged away from the quayside, reinforcing Southampton's long held claim to be the 'Gateway to the World'. A flotilla of small craft gathered to escort *Aurora* down Southampton Water while two tugs, *Redbridge* and *Lyndhurst*, were on station to guide us away with a water display.

Commemorative envelope marking *Aurora*'s maiden voyage. (*Mark Thomas collection*)

'Once the pilot disembarked at the Nab Tower, on the east coast of the Isle of Wight, we headed west into the English Channel towards the sun and fourteen nights of enjoyment ... or so we thought!

'We had table No. 31, one of the best in the Alexandria Restaurant, situated by the aft windows right in the middle of the ship. The view of the wake caused by our twenty-four knot speed was like watching a washing machine on full spin! A sumptuous meal followed and the wine flowed, the restaurant staff quietly and efficiently going about their business. After dinner, we took the opportunity to explore the ship and as we went out on deck it was evident that we were now stationary in the water. Two red lights shone from the mast, indicating the ship was not under power. It was the small hours of the morning before the problem was rectified and as we went to bed that night, we all wondered if everything was going to be alright and hoping that it was just a teething problem.

'The next morning, we were still progressing slowly, most passengers not even aware that something was wrong. Then, at 1100, Capt. Burgoine came over the public address system with the following statement, "I'm afraid I have some disappointing news. It is with great regret that I have to inform you that it is necessary to curtail this maiden voyage of *Aurora*. Damage has been sustained to a propeller shaft bearing, caused

This page: Capt. Steve Burgoine addresses passengers around the Crystal Pool on *Aurora*'s maiden voyage. (*Andrew Sassoli-Walker*)

Mark and Nicola Thomas celebrated their wedding anniversary on board *Aurora* on the maiden voyage. (*Andrew Sassoli-Walker*)

Running on one engine, *Aurora* limps home from the aborted maiden voyage. (*Andrew Sassoli-Walker*)

by overheating, and it is essential that repairs are undertaken as quickly as possible. This work can only be carried out with the ship out of service. This situation is totally unforeseen despite *Aurora* having been rigorously tested before entering service ... Further broadcasts will be made shortly regarding all arrangements for the remainder of the day."

'Everyone's hearts sank, and there was silence as we absorbed the bad news, but then, as only the British can, a Dunkirk-style spirit started to envelope the ship, especially when passengers were told they would receive a full refund, a free cruise and complimentary alcohol while on board. It was estimated that the whole affair cost P&O Cruises in the region of £8 million, but the efficient way they handled the situation very quickly averted a public relations disaster. It was extremely disappointing but everyone made sure they made the most of the last night on board. What should have been the Captain's Welcome Aboard Party became a Farewell Party, and I imagine Capt. Burgoine was filled with some trepidation as he arrived but when the Cruise Director, Phil Raymond, started to introduce

"Quick! Find the captain, tell him the chief engineer's got it going again."

The press had a field day over *Aurora's* aborted maiden voyage and trials around the Isle of Wight to see if it could be repaired, (*Southern Daily Echo*)

him, he only had time to say sorry, before an immense round of applause came from everyone gathered around the Crystal Pool.

'Wednesday dawned cold and grey, as if in sympathy with the ship. Those of us who stayed up all night watched our low key, subdued arrival back into the port that had given us such a rousing send-off only a day and a half previously. The press were there in force, of course, and a helicopter circled us as we berthed. Reporters gathered around the arrivals area trying to get good stories to make the headlines. However, they must have been disappointed, as the majority acknowledged it was beyond anyone's

control, and that the compensation package from P&O Cruises was more than generous. It was a sad sight watching the ship pass by my house as she left for dry-dock repairs at the Blohm & Voss yard in Hamburg.'

James Cusick recalls, 'During the morning of the sudden and unexpected return to Southampton there was a lady passenger who accosted port presenter Bill Alison, demanding to talk to the purser! When Bill asked what it was in connection with, she said the cancellation of the cruise, to which Bill replied, Madam, one cannot complain one can only make a comment! A priceless line in my book!' He continued, 'I recall sailing out on the maiden voyage with all the pomp and ceremony – the officers in their full blues uniform – bands playing, a flotilla of seagoing craft of all shapes and sizes, well-wishers at every viewing point between Southampton Docks and the Isle of Wight! The decks of *Aurora* were lined with excited passengers sipping champagne and dressed to the nines looking forward to the maiden voyage. How strange only a few days later to be on the Promenade Deck when *Aurora* sailed out for the Hamburg shipyard. There was only myself and Srikanth, the Accommodation Supervisor, on the deck – nobody to wave at us – contractors on board covering up the Wilton pile carpets and putting the dust covers back. It seemed unreal. Never did we think after all the preparation that we would be in this situation. After arriving in Hamburg we had ten days until *Aurora* sailed back to Southampton for her second cruise which was to many the real maiden voyage. All the crew remained on board so we opened up The Orangery for messing, the Masquerade Night Club for a disco and The Champions Bar. The staff got a good rest after the big build up, but they were soon bored and raring to get *Aurora* up and running.' *Aurora* returned to Southampton on 15 May 2000, and resumed her programme of cruises with her second scheduled cruise – a voyage to the Canary Islands.

This page: Out of the mist, a fully repaired *Aurora* returns in preparation for the second voyage, May 2000. (*Andrew Sassoli-Walker*)

The elegant Reception Desk at the bottom of the atrium on *Aurora*. (*Andrew Sassoli-Walker*)

The Crow's Nest bar on *Aurora*, with floor-to-ceiling windows offering unparalleled views forward over the bow. (*Andrew Sassoli-Walker*)

This page: Anderson's (named after Arthur Anderson, one of the founders of the Peninsular & Oriental Steam Navigation Co.) on *Aurora* was designed to give the feeling of a traditional London club, with comfortable chairs and sofas, rugs and a long bar. (*Andrew Sassoli-Walker*)

A performer's view from the stage of *Aurora's* Curzon Theatre. (*Andrew Sassoli-Walker*)

Aurora returning to Southampton at dawn, September 2009. (*Andrew Sassoli-Walker*)

Chapter 8

CHARTING THEIR COURSE

Almost from launch, both ships have attracted a loyal following. Their similarities include spectacular four-deck high atriums, each with stunning water features falling the full four decks. These are computer-controlled and automatically switch off in rough seas to avoid splashing carpets and passengers. The libraries in both ships are furnished with pieces specially commissioned from David Linley, including book and library tables, occasional chairs and the lecterns that hold a World Atlas so passengers may follow the progress of the voyage.

Where *Oriana* has the Peninsular and Oriental restaurants, named after the company itself, those on *Aurora* are called the Medina (a link with P&O's earliest routes to Moorish Spain and Portugal) and the Alexandria after the Egyptian port on their route to India. An innovation on *Aurora* was Café Bordeaux, a French-style bistro open twenty-four hours a day providing a congenial alternative to The Orangery buffet or main dining rooms. This is now a Marco Pierre White Restaurant in the evenings but remains an open seating bistro at all other times. Another alternative daytime dining option on *Aurora* was the Sidewalk Café, serving light grill-style meals and pizzas.

The hub of both ships is the bridge, where everything can be monitored. There are eleven deck officers, divided into three watches – four hours on, eight hours off. Four officers are on duty during the busier periods with one fewer on the 1200 to 1600 watch.

While the deck, engine and technical staff keep the ship running smoothly, it is the hotel department that the passengers have the most contact with. On *Aurora* almost six hundred officers and crew are under the command of the Executive Purser (a new job title brought in for *Aurora*'s launch). It is his job, together with the Food and Beverage, Accommodation and Passenger Services Managers, to make sure passengers have everything they require for a great cruise, from good food and well-stocked bars to clean and comfortable cabins. It is also the responsibility of the Executive Purser to deal with customs and immigration officers and port agents throughout a cruise.

This page, clockwise from top left: View from *Oriana*'s bridge over the Direction Finder to the bow and crew swimming pool. (*Lindsay Petrie*)

With Southampton Water like glass, *Oriana* and *Aurora* bring passengers home at the end of another cruise. (*Andrew Sassoli-Walker*)

The library on *Aurora*, with furniture by David Linley, April 2011. (*Sharon Poole*)

Grandfather clock designed and built by David Linley for the Thackeray Room on *Oriana*. (*Andrew Sassoli-Walker*)

These pages, from top left: The Peninsular Restaurant on *Oriana*. (*Andrew Sassoli-Walker*)

The Medina Restaurant on *Aurora*, Christmas 2008. (*Sharon Poole*)

The Riviera Pool on *Oriana*, flanked by plenty of open deck space for sun-loving passengers. (*Mark Engelbretson*)

Opposite Page: The Riviera Pool on *Aurora* was sunk lower into the deck than on *Oriana* to allow sunbathing terraces to be built around it. (*Mark Englebretson*)

Capt. David Pembridge in the captain's chair on the bridge of *Aurora*, 24 July 2011. (*Andrew Sassoli-Walker*)

Part of the main galley on *Aurora*. (The Ship's Photographer)

The catering department is one of the most complicated on board. On both *Oriana* and *Aurora* there is one huge galley situated between the two main restaurants and spanning the width of the ship. This is separated into specific areas such as bakery, hot area, cold area, vegetables, meat, etc. There are two other galleys, one for the buffet restaurant and another for the crew and officers' messes. *Aurora* also has a smaller galley attached to Café Bordeaux.

On *Aurora* around 7,500 meals have to be provided every day just for the passengers; add on the crew and it becomes an even greater challenge. There are well over a hundred galley crew, from the Executive Pastry Chef and sous chefs to butchers, bakers and utility hands, all reporting to one man – the Executive Chef. Among the team are also three special dietary chefs to cater for special requirements such as low-salt or diabetic food.

One of the laundry chutes on *Aurora* from the accommodation decks down to the ship's laundry on Deck One. (The Ship's Photographer)

With so many different types of bread and rolls to provide every day – typically white, wholemeal, granary, croissants, burger buns, brioche, etc., as well as pastry for tarts and desserts depending on that day's menus – the bakery team under the Head Baker work from 2000 hrs until 0800 hrs the following morning.

Stores are brought on board on pallets and then moved by fork-lift truck to the specialist storage areas on the two lowest decks. There are temperature-controlled storerooms for different products – freezers, cold store, larders, etc., even a special store for cheese, maintained at 3 degrees celsius. Fish and meat are kept separate as are white and red meat. On Deck three are the bonded store rooms for alcohol and tobacco. Passengers drink up to 8,000 bottles of wine alone. Add in beer and spirits and that is a whole lot of alcohol! When *Oriana* and *Aurora* were built

it was normal to carry sufficient food and drink for one extra cruise as a backup, but nowadays they usually only carry a few additional days' worth. On a world cruise some stores are sent ahead in containers to various ports of call.

The ships take on around 165 tons of stores on a turnaround day in Southampton. This consists of approximately 28 tons of vegetables, 3½ tons of fish, 1,000 gallons of ice cream, 14½ tons of meat and 33,000 bottles of beer. All for one fourteen day cruise! A well-rehearsed system sees a constant stream of vehicles bringing all manner of goods, with everything loaded in time for the usual 1630 hrs departure.

One of the most important, if unseen, parts of a cruise ship is the laundry. This is situated on the lowest deck and operates all day, every day. All washing – bed linen, towels, bath robes, etc. – is sent down chutes connected to all fourteen decks, straight to the laundry for sorting and washing.

One thing passengers often forget is that the ship is home to some 800 crew (fewer on *Oriana*, more on *Aurora*). Decks two to five have crew accommodation, among other things. The lowest ranks share two-berth en-suite cabins on decks two and three, while officers, according to their rank, have single or two-berth cabins, either inside or outside. Department heads and the captain have two-room suites. There is a large crew recreation room with dance floor and bar as well as their own library and gymnasium.

Katy Foxwell, then Katy Morgan, was secretary to the POSH Club, P&O Cruises' loyalty club at the time, during the years of *Oriana*'s gestation and birth. The POSH Club was named after the supposed tradition of choosing cabins on the coolest side of the ship (in the days before air conditioning) when travelling to and from India – port out, starboard home – and people paid a membership fee to join, unlike its successors the Portunus and Peninsular Clubs. She writes, 'My career with P&O Cruises spanned

Right: Katy Foxwell (neé Morgan), ex-secretary of the POSH Club, pictured on *Oriana* on her call at Honolulu as part of the world cruise, 2012. Katy now resides in Hawaii. (*Katy Foxwell*)

Far right: Countdown to Oriana magazines, maiden season brochure and documentation for pre-naming ceremony tours. (*Andrew Sassoli-Walker collection*)

the years of 1986–1997 and began when the company was located in Aldgate in London's East End. In those days, we had typewriters as the computer revolution was newly upon us. I lived through the chapter in the company's history when *Sea Princess* left the fleet of then only two ships to join Princess Cruises. Reflecting that, the company changed its name to Canberra Cruises only to revert back to P&O Cruises as we grew the fleet again and moved the London office to New Oxford Street. During this period, ten instalments of the *Countdown to Oriana* magazine led up to her much anticipated launch in April 1995. These helped endear her to the hearts of P&O Cruises' devotees who followed closely the years of her construction. *Sea Princess* was reintroduced to the P&O Cruises fleet and ultimately renamed *Victoria* and our beloved *Canberra* sadly was withdrawn from service in 1997. That period was eloquently summed

up for me in a watercolour painted by maritime and landscape artist Andrew Dibben of Norfolk. It shows *Canberra*, *Oriana* and *Victoria*, and is entitled *I Saw Three Ships Come Sailing By* (see page 70) which was the summation of my P&O Cruises cherished experience and became the cover for the Christmas card I sent out to members in 1995.'

'The binding element through these changes was The POSH Club. I am astounded now as I reflect on its remarkably generous offerings and incentives presented to entice members to sail. The POSH Club regalia was selected by Len Stuckey, another legend in P&O Cruises' land-based operation, and custom-made products and gifts by companies like Carrs, Frette, and Royal Doulton were given to members, who no doubt still proudly possess these treasures! We offered "sail and stay" holidays worldwide, escorted POSH Club themed cruises with complimentary shore excursions and exclusive parties on board, and stayed in touch

Left: Damage to a cabin bulkhead, caused by the huge wave that struck *Oriana* when she was answering a distress call from a Canadian yacht, September 2000. (*David Jewkes*)

Below: Jacqueline and Bill Arnold boarding *Aurora* in Hong Kong for part of her maiden world cruise, 2011. (*Jacqueline Arnold*)

"at home" with countrywide sales presentations and sherry receptions through the winter months, the quarterly newsletter publication, *Lookout*, and annual Christmas lunch at the Marriott at Grosvenor Square. I was privileged to be The POSH Club Secretary during this era and I look back on those truly halcyon days at sea and ashore with the greatest affection.'

The ocean can be a dangerous place and both *Oriana* and *Aurora* have rendered aid on many an occasion. In October 1999, *Oriana* crew rescued a capsized jet-skier off the Spanish coast after he was spotted by two passengers. The following May a more dramatic rescue took place when *Oriana* responded to an SOS call from a capsized Turkish cargo boat, *Orsay,* in the Mediterranean between Italy and Sicily. Nine sailors were found clinging to a raft and were rescued by crew using the fast rescue craft and were taken to Brindisi.

On 29 September 2000, while en route from New York to Southampton, *Oriana* altered course to go to the aid of a de-masted Canadian yacht. *Oriana* was subsequently stood down when a container ship, *Atlantic Companion,* arrived on scene, but then was asked for assistance once again as the container ship was having problems evacuating the crew. *Oriana* was at this point 600 miles west of Cork, Ireland, with the captain being informed of the situation, when a freak wave of some forty-feet hit her beam-on during a force ten gale. It shattered windows and flooded six passenger cabins. Running repairs were hastily carried out by the engineering team headed by Chief Engineer David Jewkes.

In 2001, while sailing through the Taiwan Strait on her first world cruise, *Aurora* was asked to assist the Cambodian ship *Pamela Dream*, which had capsized in rough seas. At the time a crewmember described the seas as 'very rough, with waves of about five metres'. *Aurora* launched her fast rescue boats and was able to retrieve three survivors. Unfortunately during the rescue one of *Aurora*'s propellers was damaged by the floating wreckage, and had to be repaired in Singapore.

In 2005 *Aurora* responded to a call for help from a fifty-one foot yacht – the *Grandee*, which was in trouble in gale force winds off the Dorset coast. A member of the yacht's crew had fallen overboard, and although he had luckily been recovered by the time *Aurora* arrived, the liner stayed in position to provide shelter and act as a radio relay for the coastguard helicopter while the injured man was airlifted off. She then escorted the yacht back to Poole where she could hand her charge over to the coastguard.

Since P&O Cruises' ships are based in the UK, their guests are ninety-nine per cent British, but there is the occasional passenger from overseas. As previously mentioned, Carl Ilardi travelled with a group of around ten Americans to New York in 2000. He recalls, 'Shortly after we got on board I went to the restaurant to check our table. A couple of elderly English ladies were ahead of me in the queue talking. One must have felt that she was safely surrounded by compatriots as she was telling her companion about friends of hers, "They're American but really very nice". I couldn't resist chiming in with, "Sometimes we are even well behaved". A bit embarrassed she turned to me, "Oh, I'm really terribly sorry, I didn't mean ..." "That's quite alright, don't worry about it," I smiled. Let our English holiday begin.'

On 1 September 2001, *Aurora* set off on a nine-night cruise to the USA arriving first at Boston on 7 September before sailing into New York on 9 September. While most passengers then flew home, others stayed in New York for six days of sightseeing while *Aurora* ran a series of short US charters. On 15 September she was due to sail home on a 10-night cruise, calling first at Newport, Rhode Island, Boston and Bar Harbour, Maine. On the fateful day of 11 September 2001, when the two hijacked aeroplanes were flown into the World Trade Centre in New York City, *Aurora* was at sea. Instead of returning to New York as scheduled for 15 September, she was re-routed to Boston. Those passengers in New York hotels were

Hannah Watts. aged 9

Menu cover for *Aurora*'s first birthday dinner, designed by Hannah Watts, aged nine. It has been autographed by Tom O'Connor, who was the headline entertainer on board. (*Michael Whittingham collection*)

It has become a personal tradition that the P&O Cruises agent Aslak Lefdal presents a stag's head to a ship on their maiden call at Olden, Norway. Sven, as the stag is now called, has pride of place on the bridge of *Oriana*. (*Sharon Poole*)

taken by road to join *Aurora* there. The ship then sailed to Halifax, Nova Scotia, to pick up some more passengers who were stranded while on the Eastern Canada shore tour, as well as some entertainers and staff, including two chaplains from the UK. She then sailed for Southampton. Another company ship, *Royal Princess*, was the last cruise ship to sail out of New York before the attacks twelve hours later.

In August 2007 *Aurora* arrived back in Southampton from a cruise to the Greek Islands with tender No. 8 missing! It had been the subject of all the on-board jokes since they had had to leave it behind in Corfu, with one entertainer apparently giving a hilarious rendition of Elvis Presley's *Return to Sender*, re-written as *Return my Tender*. Although funny from a passenger's perspective, the incident itself was much more serious. During the day in Corfu there had been a crew drill. While winching the tender back on board, the rear hook failed and several crew members inside the tender were injured. Capt. Charlie Carr gave an announcement that *Aurora* would be late leaving Corfu while they tried to lift the tender onto the foredeck. This meant dismantling the crew sports deck so, instead of participating in the 1960s/70s night in Masquerade, many passengers

were crammed on the front observation decks watching proceedings. Daniel Newland takes up the story. 'At about 2330hrs, after some hours waiting for a crane (ever tried finding a large crane on a bank holiday evening?), and then beginning to lift the tender, they decided that the operation was too risky and it was aborted. Capt. Carr said we could still sail with one tender missing, although there were the usual shipboard rumours such as people being offloaded as the ship could not sail at full capacity with one tender lifeboat missing! At 0100hrs we sailed for Gibraltar and still got there a few hours early.'

During the 2009 World Cruise, *Aurora* again experienced problems with her propulsion system shortly after leaving Sydney, Australia. She continued on to Auckland, New Zealand, to undergo repairs, leaving for Hawaii on 12 March 2009.

In 2005, *Oriana* celebrated ten years in service, having carried nearly half a million passengers to over 295 ports all over the world. The following year she underwent a £12 million refit and refurbishment in the Lloyd Werft yard in Bremerhaven, Germany. The popular but underused Curzon Room was turned into a Gary Rhodes fine-dining venue, following his success with a similar venture on *Arcadia*. All the decorative features of the room were retained such as the magnificent chandeliers and the wall tapestries, but the piano was moved to the Pacific Lounge and at the same time Tiffany's Bar was upgraded with new curtains and lighting to provide an intimate pre- and post-dinner piano bar. The new restaurant was also provided with its own galley. The new look did not stop there. The Lord's Tavern sports bar was extended and given large-screen plasma televisions and a new sound system while its slot machines were moved to the casino. The children's areas too were redesigned and given new facilities such as electronic game machines. The cabins were also refurbished with new bedding, curtains and carpets as part of P&O Cruises Elevation programme. At this time she was re-flagged to Hamilton, Bermuda, so that weddings could be performed on board.

John Bull and his wife Sandra are no strangers to life at sea. John, a steward in his younger years with both Cunard and Union Castle, met Sandra while she was sailing home to Southampton from Cape Town. It was while serving with Cunard that the quote 'Every meal a banquet, every Steward a movie star' became known, but John reiterated that this comment is still as relevant now, and equally applicable on P&O Cruises' ships as on Cunard, with the exemplary levels of service offered, such as the staff's incredible capacity for not only remembering names but also one's favourite tipple, as well as other preferences.

While on board *Oriana* celebrating Sandra's sixtieth birthday, there were in the region of thirty waiters singing 'Happy Birthday' to her. With so many days spent on board, many of the crew are well known to them, and John has even been known to offer them home-cooked meals at his Southampton home on turnaround days! One crew member even referred to him as 'Royal Mr Bull Sir' – a sign of the regard both crew and passengers have for each other within the P&O Cruises 'family'.

From top left: Oriana in dry dock for maintenance and refit. (The Ship's Photographer)

Marco Pierre White's new Ocean Grill on *Oriana*, situated in the original Curzon Room, November 2011. (P&O Cruises)

The striking Tiffany-style glass ceiling at the top of the atrium on *Oriana*, reflected in the piano in Tiffany's Bar. (*Andrew Sassoli-Walker*)

Lisa and Steve Hatfull with Capt. David Pembridge, after their wedding on board *Oriana*, 8 November 2008. (*Lisa Hatfull*)

This pages: The stunning view from the cable car over Funchal, Madeira with *Oriana* berthed in the harbour, November 2007. (*Andrew Sassoli-Walker*)

Aurora seen from the stern of *Oriana* in Funchal, Madeira when both ships were on Christmas cruises, 2010. (*Jeanette Fluellen*)

Oriana and *Aida Blu* berthed bow to bow in Funchal, Madeira, November 2007. (*Andrew Sassoli-Walker*)

Funchal in Madeira is one of their favourite ports as it was a stopover port on the Union Castle run between the UK and South Africa. In those days, the ship would anchor off, and young boys on bum boats would sail out to the ship with Madeiran souvenirs that would be hoisted aboard via a heaving line. In return, passengers would throw coins over the side and these young boys would then dive down to collect them. New Year's Eve 2010 saw Sandra and John on board *Oriana* for the traditional firework

This page: Sophie and Bethany Englebretson with crew member Elvis Dias, on *Oriana*, April 2008. Elvis was one of the crew members who helped to look after Sophie when her mother was taken ill on board *Aurora*, when Sophie was six months old. (*Mark Engelbretson*)

Aurora berthed in Antigua in the Caribbean. (*Paul Scase*)

Oriana at Half Moon Cay, March 2010. (*Gordon Vinnicombe*)

New Year's Eve deck party in the Caribbean on *Oriana*. (*Eileen Wilson*)

celebrations in Funchal. Also alongside was *Artemis*, with *Queen Victoria* vacating her berth and going to anchor so *Oriana* could come alongside. Their last day at sea on that cruise proved just how the Bay of Biscay can show its kind face even in winter, with them both sitting on the aft deck till tea time on 7 January 2011, a perfect relaxing end to yet another cruise.

Far left: Aft deck and wake of *Aurora*, with the Terrace Pool a venue for a Greasy Pole competition. (*Paul Newland*)

Left: The RNLI Torbay Severn Class lifeboat *Alec & Christina Dykes* approaching *Aurora* to evacuate a sick passenger, 19 September 2011. *Aurora* was on passage to New York when Capt. Neil Turnbull made the decision, in consultation with medical and shore based staff, to call for assistance to get the patient to hospital ashore. *Aurora* altered course to meet the lifeboat off Berry Head where the patient and their family were safely evacuated at 0200hrs and taken to Torbay Hospital. P&O Cruises and the individual ships make regular donations to the RNLI. (RNLI/Nigel Millard)

Right: Santa Claus emerges from the funnel of *Oriana*, Christmas Day 2010. (*Jeanette Fluellen*)

Far right: The atrium on *Aurora*, decorated for Christmas, 2008. (*Sharon Poole*)

This page, from top left: Oriana at the Mayflower Terminal in Southampton immediately after her refit when the aft sponson or ducktail was fitted, November 2011. (*Andrew Sassoli-Walker*)

The Sorrento Restaurant on *Oriana*, created during the refit in November 2011. (P&O Cruises)

Bow wash from *Oriana* on a sunny morning in the Mediterranean. (*Gordon Vinnicombe*)

Oriana alongside at Vigo. This image clearly illustrates the liner heritage in the shape of her bow. (*Andrew Sassoli-Walker*)

Aurora and *Oriana* together in Southampton. (*Andrew Sassoli-Walker*)

Thsese pages: Oriana in St Maarten. Once one of the largest cruise ships in the world, she is now dwarfed by her companions – *Sea Princess, Carnival Dream and Grand Princess* and on the right, *Oasis of the Seas* and *Celebrity Solstice*. (*Zak Coombs*)

Oriana at Kotor, Montenegro, 28 April 2010. (*Lindsay Petrie*)

Aurora, berthed in the tranquillity of Eidfjord, Norway, 2009. (*Stuart McGregor*)

Oriana tendering passengers ashore at Andalnes, Norway, 2006. (*Stuart McGregor*)

Mark Englebretson, currently Head of Group Pensions at Carnival UK also has reason to regard both ships, but particularly *Oriana*, with affection. It was while cruising on board her in 2002 that he and his wife Nicola discovered they were expecting their first child. When their daughter was born Mark even asked his wife if they could name her Oriana to a resounding No! Their daughter was duly christened Sophie. Sophie's first cruise was on *Aurora* on what proved to be a rather eventful voyage. Nicola unfortunately ended up in the ship's hospital, but the stewards and crew rallied round Mark to help him look after Sophie, then aged six months. Sophie also learned to swim for the first time on board *Oriana* while crossing the Atlantic to the Caribbean in 2008 – a cruise remembered for the rare sighting of a blue whale close to the ship.

Speaking of wildlife, Laura Lake also recalled a particularly memorable moment on board *Aurora*. 'It took place when I was working in the tour office for part of *Aurora*'s world cruise in March 2004 and we were sailing from Singapore to Mumbai, rather a long five days at sea! I was on my lunch break catching some sun on the aft of the ship by the terrace pool and I heard someone shout 'dolphins!' With that I jumped up from my lounger and looking over the stern saw the dolphins playing in the wake – a pod of well over a hundred. They were clearly aware that they had an audience and started jumping out and showing off as well as trying to swim faster than the ship. It was a fantastic sight as before that I had only ever seen them in parks like Seaworld. It is something that will always remind me of *Aurora* and the wonderful deck space at the stern which allowed me to see them so closely.'

In late November 2011, *Oriana* sailed to Germany for a major refit. During this yard time she underwent a number of changes and improvements. Most noticeably a sponson or duck-tail was added to her stern. This increases stability and allows more flexibility when loading. *Oriana* was to become exclusively for adults on her return to cruising. This has been a popular option with P&O Cruises' passengers on *Artemis* and *Arcadia*. Since *Artemis* left the fleet in 2011, to be replaced by the much smaller *Adonia*, it was felt another vessel was required to meet the high demand for such ships. To this end the area once given over to children's entertainment was converted into additional cabins, including two single cabins and twelve balcony staterooms. The *Oriana* Rhodes restaurant was changed to Marco Pierre White's Ocean Grill and part of The Conservatory now becomes the Italian themed restaurant Sorrento in the evening.

Chapter 9

AN ENGINEER'S DREAM

P&O Cruises traditionally expect a life span of around twenty to twenty-five years from their new ships, so they are designed and built with future needs and expectations in mind, utilising as much state-of-the-art technology as is available at the time. Mostly this involves a gradual evolution of systems but in some instances the timing of when a new vessel enters service can mean it becomes more of a great leap forward. In many ways, *Oriana* was one such ship.

Jim Hunter recalls, 'P&O Cruises took me on board, under contract, about three months after the contract with Meyer-Werft was signed. Selection of engine and other equipment manufacturers was yet to take place but the type of propulsion system – diesel direct-drive with controllable pitch propellers and electrical boost – had already been agreed with the shipyard and was included in the contract specification. Diesel-mechanical is a more efficient system as the ship has pairs of engines, large and small, commonly known as a father and son arrangement. This gives enormous flexibility as to how the engines are run, and by

only using the appropriate engines for the required output, some can be temporarily shut down, thus saving fuel. However, this is a very complex system, and diesel-electric engines which power electric motors are more commonplace.' It is this complexity which led Capt. Alastair Clark to comment that *Oriana* was an engineer's dream!

David Jewkes is a Chief Engineer with P&O Cruises. He explained that, 'Both *Oriana* and *Aurora* are very similar to manage when it comes down to outside of the machinery spaces. In other words the hotel sides have roughly the same demand on power. When it comes to the engine rooms, *Oriana* is a direct-drive ship and *Aurora* is diesel-electric. *Aurora* has four engines which generate electricity which is used to power the ship's hotel and main motors. In the case of *Oriana*, she has quite a complex power plant arrangement. She has father and son engine arrangements which drive the propeller shafts via clutches and gearboxes. She also has four off generators which generate the power required for the hotel but which can also provide boost power for the propulsion. The propulsion can even

Right: The Engine Control Room on *Oriana*. (*David Jewkes*)

Far right: The Engine Control Room on *Aurora*, c. 2001. (The Ship's Photographer)

provide power for the hotel via shaft-driven generators. *Oriana's* power management is thus much more complex than *Aurora*. If you have an issue with one of the father engines you lose 50 per cent of the propulsion power of that shaft as a result. In the case of *Aurora* if you have one of the four main engines out you only lose 25 per cent of the total generating power, 12½ per cent per shaft and thus equal shaft power loss. One does learn to love *Oriana* however because she is so much more of a challenge to maintain and master, which engineers like.

David went on to explain more about the decision in 1999 to reverse the rotation of the twin propellers to reduce the vibration from which *Oriana* had suffered from launch. 'When Lord Sterling commissioned *Oriana* he wanted a ship which was very manoeuvrable as well as fast so that she could get down through the Bay to the warmer weather of the Mediterranean quickly, and could manoeuvre into small constricted ports.

This influenced the choice of direct-drive controllable-pitch propellers. These would give the manoeuvrability required but unusually, they were rotated outboard in order to achieve higher powers. This was not the normal rotation for controllable-pitch props and caused the higher than normal vibration at high speed during *Oriana's* early years of service. Between her launch in 1995 and 1999 experts looked at all options in order to try and reduce the vibration. They concluded that the best way was to reverse the direction of rotation of the propellers. This would take the ship out of service for approximately three weeks. All that was required was to swap all the running gear from the port to starboard side and vice versa. This sounds simple but in reality involves taking out all the running gear in each engine. In the gear boxes the gear wheels had to be changed since they are cut and formed in one driven direction. Finally the port and starboard propellers were switched over. After all this work,

Above left: The propeller shafts being switched over on *Oriana* to try and resolve the cavitation issue, 1999. (*David Jewkes*)

Above right: Lifting the replacement crankshaft into *Oriana,* July 2004. (*Caryll Young*)

during the sea trials after the reversal, we wiped the starboard propeller main shaft bearing. This meant that we had to go back into dry dock and take the shafts out and re-metal both bearings port and starboard. This also meant cancelling two further cruises. We re-designed the bearings and re-entered service a couple of weeks late. Most importantly, the vibration levels were now at an acceptable level.

In July 2004 *Oriana* suffered a major mechanical problem when, just as they were leaving Palma, the No.2 engine suffered an over-speed causing major damage to the port crankshaft which began running out of true. As *Oriana* limped back to Southampton, it was decided to attempt to replace the crankshaft with the vessel still in service, something never before tried. The versatile configuration of her engines meant that, so long as she didn't need to steam at over 21 knots, she could function perfectly adequately on the remaining engines. The engineering team, together with Lloyd Werft engineers and heavy-lifting experts, dismantled the engine while in Southampton on 14 August. They removed the pistons, cylinder heads, turbo charger and flywheel before lifting the engine, weighing some 200 tons, up 2 metres on hydraulic jacks. The damaged crankshaft was then removed and laid to one side and the ship left as normal on a Mediterranean cruise. In Palma, two cranes were on the dockside to assist in lifting the old crankshaft up through the engineering hatch and out onto the dockside before performing the same manoeuvre in reverse to get the new part down into the engine room. At the tightest point there was just 2 mm clearance. The new crankshaft was then secured until the ship reached Naxos where the engine was reassembled. Men from Lloyds Register met *Oriana* at Venice to check the running of the new part and certificate it and *Oriana* completed her cruise with four working engines again. It was an immense achievement for all involved.

Aurora's two well-known mechanical failures were both unfortunate, and unforeseeable.

The first was the failed propeller bearing that curtailed her maiden voyage. Advance warning of this might have been spotted had it not been for the sea temperature. *Aurora*'s extensive sea trials were in the cold North Sea where the viscosity of the oil was greater therefore masking the growing problem. In fact *Aurora* passed with flying colours even though they encountered some severe weather, much as with *Oriana* five years previously. However, as *Aurora* moved to the milder English Channel, the oil viscosity grew less, until eventually metal was rubbing on metal, causing the widely publicised failure.

It was felt that the only solution was to dry dock the ship and replace the failed components. Fortunately Blohm & Voss in Hamburg were able to take on the work at short notice and *Aurora* was ready for her advertised second cruise – twelve nights to the Canary Islands.

The second, more spectacular failure happened in 2005. *Aurora* was on her run back to Southampton from Madeira at the end of the Christmas Cruise. She was due to turn around in Southampton on 9 January and then head out on her world cruise, which would take her down to the Falklands and around South America. Over 1,000 passengers were booked for the full world cruise with many more sailing on sectors. On her way home up the Portuguese coast the starboard propulsion electric motor (PEM) tripped and could not be reset. She completed the journey on one engine and arrived at Southampton at 2200 on the evening of 9 January, some sixteen hours later than scheduled.

Once in port, a wealth of expertise was called on to try and resolve the issue. Richard Vie was among those called in from the technical team ashore. Every possible avenue was explored and although repairs could be effected the motor could only be used on very limited power with no guarantee of lasting for very long. After several days and trials round the Isle of Wight (much to the amusement of the press watching the situation with interest) the decision was made to take the ship out of service, dry-dock her in Bremerhaven and replace both main propulsion motors, something which had never been done before.

Looking back, Richard feels it might have been possible to trim the propeller blades, thus lessening the load on the motor and enabling the ship to continue. This could be done by specialist divers. However, in view of the fact that the ship was sailing on a world cruise and could be away from land for long periods, it was felt this would be a risky option and that dry-docking would be safer and provide a long-term solution. By keeping everyone informed, and offering a generous compensation package, passengers accepted the situation with disappointment but good grace, much to the frustration of the press who lined the dockside at disembarkation, eager for some lively and controversial quotes! Rather than let it go to waste, P&O Cruises donated the three and a half tonnes of fresh fruit and vegetables from her stores to a Southampton charity that worked to relive hardship and poverty. Most of her officers and crew were flown home, redeployed to other ships or shore-based at Southampton temporarily.

Chief Engineer David Jewkes: 'Once the decision was made we were all relieved as we could then focus on the job in hand – changing the motors. *Crown Princess* was under construction in Italy and her engines were near identical so we took those and used them in *Aurora*. It was not

Above: Damage caused by the winding failures in *Aurora's* engines. (*David Jewkes*)

Far right: Removing part of the hull of *Aurora* to remove the faulty engine. (*David Jewkes*)

Opposite top left: David Jewkes (on the left in this picture) was Chief Engineer when *Aurora* had to abort her world cruise and head to Germany for an engine change. He recalled, 'Obviously we should have been in a warm climate and exotic places, not freezing cold and not even afloat. Morale was good but it did start to falter slightly as the days and weeks went by. In order to get the lads together and for a little team building I got them all up on deck for a snow ball fight and to build a snow man. At first they all thought I had cracked up but did as I asked. Once the first snow ball had been thrown the rest just fell into place. We had about forty-five minutes of pure fun.' (*David Jewkes*)

a straight swap however; we had to use some parts from the old motors along with parts from the new ones. Even acquiring the motors from the *Crown* was not a straightforward issue, as technically they were not ours to take. The ship was being built for Princess Cruises by the shipyard who at that stage owned the part-built ship. Negotiations had to take place with the yard as taking the motors could delay delivery of *Crown Princess* and they were under stiff penalty if that occurred! Then we had the problem of transporting the motors from Italy to Germany as they were too big to be driven. They needed to be shipped and quickly. The old motors, or rather what was left after some components were re-used, were scrapped as they were totally beyond repair. The whole issue was a huge challenge which, as I said previously, engineers adore. The *Aurora* motor failure and replacement was a monumental undertaking of which I was very proud to be a part. I could talk about it for days!'

Suffice it to say, the motors were replaced, *Aurora* passed her trials and re-entered service on 22 April, at the time she was originally due to return from her world cruise. While *Aurora* was in Bremerhaven, it was decided to give parts of the vessel an early refit at the same time. Inside the ship, surfaces were repainted, carpets renewed and furniture re-upholstered where necessary. Outside, the lower hull was given a new coat of anti-fouling paint and the teak decking was sanded down, recoated and sealed. It was also decided to bring forward a few things that were originally part of the planned December refit, such as the installation of coloured lights and a sound system around the Riviera Pool, so that shows could be presented out on deck. Most importantly, a new Integrated Bridge System was installed. With improved electronic charts and radar system it gave the bridge crew more navigational information and *Aurora* was able to take her place once again as one of the most technologically advanced ships afloat.

Top right: The engines being lifted from the building dock of *Crown Princess,* to be transported to Germany and installed into *Aurora.* (*David Jewkes*)

Bottom left: Rebuilding *Aurora's* engines. (*David Jewkes*)

Bottom right: The new motors from *Crown Princess* arriving ready to be installed into *Aurora.* (*David Jewkes*)

Far left: The central command console with new Integrated Bridge System on the bridge of *Aurora*. (*Andrew Sassoli-Walker*)

Left: Sorting waste for recycling in the garbage area on Deck 2, *Aurora*. (The Ship's Photographer)

As these issues illustrate, a chief engineer rarely has a 'normal' working day.

David Jewkes explains, 'I normally rise at 0600 hrs and will be in my office by 0630 hrs. I review the power plant, night reports and e-mails before having a meeting with the senior technical officers to discuss the day's work and any issues we may have. Once the meeting is completed I will have my breakfast and then have a walk around the ship visiting the bridge, hotel areas and machinery spaces. This can easily take me up to lunch time. In the afternoon I will deal with any necessary paperwork and e-mails plus review any work which has been taking place – this could be anywhere on the vessel. I normally leave my office between 1830 hrs and 1900 hrs in the evening and then relax before getting ready for dinner with the passengers. I host a table in the restaurant on most nights and it could be that there is a cocktail party to attend prior to dinner also. Obviously if the ship is docking or sailing then I would be in the engine control room. In some ports I will be on duty in the early hours of the morning, as is the case for arrivals into Southampton as the pilotage is quite long. During the day there may also be meetings with the senior management team which consists of the captain, deputy captain and executive purser or perhaps other meetings – Cruise Meeting, Executive Committee meeting. I also have hygiene rounds or crew rounds to conduct. There is always something going on that requires my attention each and every day but I hope to be tucked up in bed not later than 2300 hrs!'

The engineering department on *Aurora* consists of eighteen engineering and electro-technical officers and three British chief petty officers, supported by forty-four Filipino fitters, technicians, motor men, waste disposal operators and wipers. Routine maintenance is done in port with one engine shut down whilst the other maintains power for the hotel side of the ship. There is even a ship's carpenter still on board, although rather than repair the hull or a mast as in days gone by, he attends to broken furniture and suchlike.

The Electro Technical Department (a department first introduced by P&O and Princess Cruises for *Royal Princess* in 1984) employs nine officers and five ratings. Their job is to maintain all on-board electrical equipment from the ship's radio to a toaster in the galley.

Chapter 10

IN CONCLUSION

Oriana and *Aurora* both continue to be held in much affection by P&O Cruises' passengers. Indeed, there are no other ships like them, due to their bespoke design. If all goes to plan, in 2015 the largest P&O Cruises ship to date will be introduced, two decades after the launch of *Oriana*. It is testament to the bold move by the company at that time to take the £200 million gamble on *Oriana*, and the subsequent introduction of *Aurora* at the turn of the twenty-first century. These two vessels played a major part in helping the cruise industry become the success it is today. It is our hope this book will not only record their history and service, but will provide a lasting souvenir of two very special ships, the like of which, considering today's cruise market and world economy, is unlikely to be built again.

APPENDIX

Statistics		Oriana	Aurora
		Oriana	*Aurora*
Yard No.		636	640
Call sign		GVSN (changed to ZCDU9 on reflagging to Bermuda)	GUSS (changed to ZCDW9 on reflagging to Bermuda)
Port of registry		1995–2006 London 2006 – Hamilton, Bermuda	2000–2007 London 2007 – Hamilton, Bermuda
IMO number		9050137	9169524
Gross tonnage		69,153	76,152

Length	260 m (853ft)	272m (886ft)
Beam	32.2m (105ft)	35.2m (106ft)
Draught	7.9m (26ft)	8.4m
Service speed	24 knots	24 knots
Maximum speed	25 knots	25 knots
Crew	760	850
Regular Passenger Capacity	1,760	1,878
Maximum Passenger Capacity	1,976	1,950
Passenger decks	10	10

On an average fourteen-day cruise, passengers get through 42,000 cakes, 4,000 litres of ice-cream and 5,880 bottles of gin.

Every day 9,000 meals are served to passengers and crew (*Aurora*)

Champagne consumed in an average year: 13,000 bottles per ship

Minimum turning circle: 463m – ¼ nautical mile at 16 knots (*Aurora*)

FIRSTS FOR *ORIANA*

In 1995 she was the largest and fastest liner built in quarter of a century.

Largest swimming pool afloat at the time of her launch.

More open deck space than any other ship afloat in 1995.

Most technologically advanced ship afloat in 1995.

In 1995 she had the largest ship's stabilisers ever built.

First ship to have low-level safety lighting in public areas.

First passenger ship to have smoke control systems.

FIRSTS FOR *AURORA*

First UK passenger ship to be allowed to use electronic navigation charts.

First P&O Cruises' ship to have the title of Executive Purser (called Chief Purser before).

First P&O Cruises' ship to have a digital x-ray machine in the medical centre.

ACKNOWLEDGEMENTS

We are indebted to everyone who has provided information, assistance and images for this book and endured our numerous questioning. In particular we would like to thank:

Carnival UK, in particular Richard Vie, Mark Engelbretson and Maurice Lowman

P&O Cruises, in particular, Michelle Baker, Zak Coombs, James Cusick, David Jewkes, Laura Lake, Tim Newman and Lindsay Petrie.

Amberley Publishing, especially Campbell McCutcheon.

RFD Beaufort/Survitec Group especially Richard McCormick and Tamara Petersen.

Southern Daily Echo, in particular Ian Murray and Jez Gale.

Other people who have provided invaluable assistance are Charles Arkinstall, Jacqueline Arnold, Heather Dove, Katy Foxwell, Comm. Ian Gibb Rtd, Gwyn Hughes, Jim Hunter, Carl Ilardi, Carola Ingall, Robert Lloyd, Alan Mackenzie, Stuart McGregor, Carol and John Porter, David Raymonde, Capt. Hamish Reid Rtd., Peter Smith, Patrick Sutcliffe, Mark Thomas, Eileen Wilson, Michael Whittingham, and all officers and crew, past and present, of *Oriana* and *Aurora*.

Opposite: November 5 fireworks over Southampton light up *Aurora*. (Andrew Sassoli-Walker)

Above: Gangway notice board – the last thing passengers see on final disembarkation. (*Andrew Sassoli-Walker*)

FURTHER READING

Cartwright, Roger, *P&O Princess – The Cruise Ships*, History Press, 2009

Ingall, Carola, *The P&O Line and Princess Cruises*, Ship Pictorial Publications 1997

Poole, Sharon & Sassoli-Walker, Andrew, *P&O Cruises: Celebrating 175 Years of Heritage*, Amberley Publishing, 2011

Quartermaine, Peter & Peter, Bruce, *Cruise, Identity, Design & Culture*, Laurence King Publishing, 2006

Aurora – Dawn of a New Era, P&O Cruises, 2000

Oriana – from Dream to Reality, P&O Cruises, 1995

Various, *The Cruise, a novel of Murder & Romance*, Studio Editions, 1995

A sunset reflected in a porthole on the promenade deck, *Oriana*. (*Andrew Sassoli-Walker*)